Charts

OF

Reformation and Enlightenment Church History

Books in the Zondervan*Charts* Series

Charts of Bible Prophecy (H. Wayne House and Randall Price)

Charts of Reformation and Enlightenment Church History (John D. Hannah)

Charts of Ancient and Medieval Church History (John D. Hannah)

Charts of Christian Theology and Doctrine (H. Wayne House)

Charts of Cults, Sects, and Religious Movements (H. Wayne House)

Charts of the Gospels and the Life of Christ (Robert L. Thomas)

Chronological and Background Charts of Church History (Robert C. Walton)

Chronological and Background Charts of the New Testament (H. Wayne House)

Chronological and Background Charts of the Old Testament (John H. Walton)

Chronological and Thematic Charts of Philosophies and Philosophers (Milton D. Hunnex)

Taxonomic Charts of Theology and Biblical Studies (M. James Sawyer)

Timeline Charts of the Western Church (Susan Lynn Peterson)

Charts

OF

Reformation and Enlightenment Church History

John D. Hannah

ZONDERVAN™

GRAND RAPIDS, MICHIGAN 49530 USA

ZONDERVAN™

Charts of Reformation and Enlightenment Church History
Copyright © 2004 by John David Hannah

Requests for information should be addressed to:
Zondervan, *Grand Rapids, Michigan 49530*

Library of Congress Cataloging-in-Publication Data

Hannah, John D.
    Charts of Reformation and Enlightenment church history / John D. Hannah.—1st ed.
      p. cm.
    ISBN 0-310-23317-8
    1. Church history—Chronology—Charts, diagrams, etc.   I. Title.
BR149.H334 2006
270.6'02'02—dc22

                                2003020807

All Scripture quotations, unless otherwise indicated, are taken from the *Holy Bible: New International Version®*. NIV®. Copyright © 1973, 1978, 1984 by International Bible Society. Used by permission of Zondervan. All rights reserved.

All rights reserved. No part of this publication may be reproduced, stored in a retrieval system, or transmitted in any form or by any means—electronic, mechanical, photocopy, recording, or any other—without the prior permission of the publisher, except as follows: Individuals may make a single copy of a chart (or a single transparency of a chart) from this book for purposes of private study, scholarship, research, or classroom use only. Teachers may make multiple copies of a chart from this book for classroom use only, not to exceed one copy per student in class.

Interior design by Robin Welsh

Printed in the United States of America

04 05 06 07 08 09 /❖ML/ 10 9 8 7 6 5 4 3 2 1

Dedication

This book is affectionately dedicated to Dr. Edwin C. Deibler (1915–2003), my mentor. For forty years he was my teacher, friend, and department chairman. I love him and miss him deeply. Heaven is richer for sure though hope of seeing him someday does not fill the emptiness his homecoming has left in my soul. Words cannot express the debt I owe.

What can I say about this man?
Who touched my life so deeply.

His greatest gifts to me were six:

His Savior to preach and adore
His love for students to teach and mold
His joy of family: wife, children, and grandchildren
His zest for living, to laugh and sing
His faith in a boy who needed the comfort of being loved
His unrelenting desire to shape and bend me.

My promise to you, choicest of fathers, in the days that remain for me are these:

I will remember your shaping, controlling love in my life
I will strive to be for others what you have been for me
I want to be remembered not as a teacher, but as one who in loving God
pointed countless others to Him.

Acknowledgments

Projects incur debts because we are not capable of doing things alone. To my wife, Carolyn, I am thankful for years of helpfulness, for her unflinching display of kindness, and for her willingness to endure hours without her mate.

To the institution I have been a part of for over thirty years, Dallas Seminary, my gratitude is difficult to express because my debt is so great. I am thankful for the vision of the leadership of the school to provide teachers with the tools necessary for the execution of the art of classroom teaching. The audiovisual department of the institution has been generous in the gift of time and efforts to make my ideas come to life. To wonderful graphic artists, I give you my thanks: Don Regier, the director of the AV department, Mary Nees (a former employee who helped in my beginning years), and Linda Tomczak. To my students throughout the years who helped me understand my ideas through constructive insights and criticism, what can I say? A special thanks goes to Brian Matz, now a graduate student at another institution, and David Largent, a current student at the seminary. To the staff of the libraries of the seminary I thank you also, particularly Jeff Webster, a consummate scholar and friend.

Finally, to a faithful and generous secretary, Mrs Beth Motley, what can I say but I appreciate your kindness and care. I thank the editorial staff of Zondervan for their interest in my work and expert literary and technical skills in making it possible. I have deeply appreciated Dirk Buursma, my editor. His letters have revealed a godly servant's heart that is a treasure to me and the Lord's church.

Contents

Charts of Reformation and Enlightenment Church History

The value of history has fallen on difficult times in contemporary culture. Postmoderns have demonstrated a tendency to disregard the past as a useless and even debilitating relic, something akin to unwanted dreams and painful experiences. Learning from the collective wisdom of the ages seems of little value in an era where technology and the sciences receive the most support from government and the arts and humanities are marginalized. We seem determined to improve our outward circumstances while allowing the inner life to decay. Great literature is not read and cherished, cultural values are nullified through the ever-changing excitement of the merely transitory, and life is tyrannized by captivating trivia. A society without a knowledge of its past is one without hope, cursed with the perception that an endless array of passing fads is meaningful. What we seem to prize most is the stuff of future garage sales, the emptiness of preoccupation with athleticism, the spiral of increased debt, and the phantom of deep relationships shattered by broken promises.

At least in part, the contemporary church seems to have imbibed the culture more than resisted its largely unbiblical values. This can be seen in the lack of awareness the Christian has of his or her heritage. With some sense of discomfort they may be enticed to articulate a vague awareness of Martin Luther or John Calvin, yet there seems to be little, if any, understanding that the Christian faith draws on a rich heritage that is centuries in its development. Part of the problem, if truth be told, is that in many of our educational institutions and churches Christians are not being grounded in their heritage.

This brings me to the purpose of preparing this volume, the second of three volumes, on the history of the Christian church. Before one bemoans the situation too loudly, or at least too incessantly, he ought to endeavor to do something about it. What I have provided are tools for the teaching of our heritage: various charts, diagrams, and maps, together with explanatory captions, unfolding the history of the church. Included with the book is a CD-ROM PowerPoint® presentation, which enhances the use of each teaching tool.

In approaching this second volume, teacher and student alike must be reminded that the history of the church cannot be neatly divided and compartmentalized. Movements have a context that precedes their appearance, and this is important to grasp if we are to achieve a more accurate understanding. The best understanding is available when the microscope of details are placed in the telescopic perspective of broad events. Simply put, movements and events (even people) have a prehistory that, at least to some degree, helps us to understand them. Therefore, it is important to view this volume in the context of the previous one. The meaning of the Reformation and the Enlightenment can most fully be appreciated when seen in the light of the events of the fourteenth and fifteenth centuries.

EARLY MODERN EUROPE AND THE REFORMATION (1500 to 1650)

The Background of the Reformation

Major Schisms in the First Sixteen Centuries

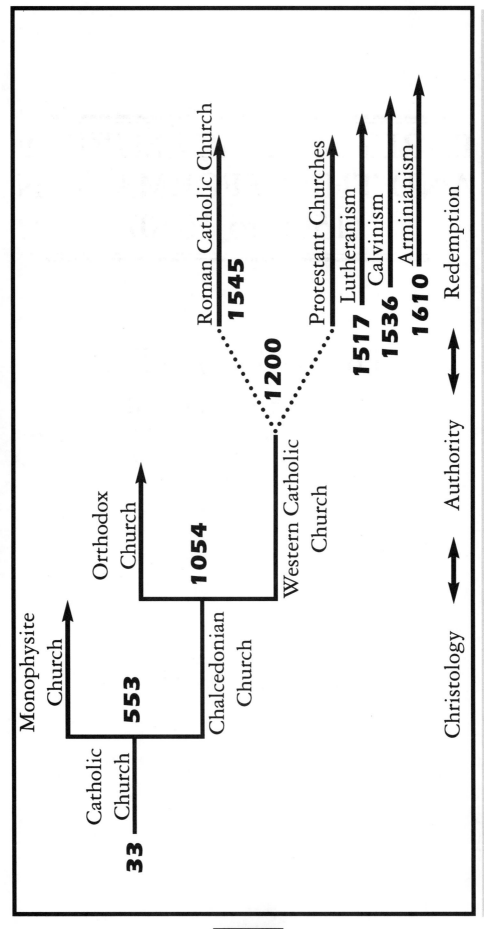

33 Catholic Church

553 Monophysite Church

Chalcedonian Church

1054 Orthodox Church

Western Catholic Church

1200 Roman Catholic Church **1545**

Protestant Churches

1517 Lutheranism
1536 Calvinism
1610 Arminianism

Christology ⟷ Authority ⟷ Redemption

In the sixth century, the debate concerning the relationship of the divine and human capacities in Christ divided Christendom (See vol. 1, charts 77–81). The Chalcedonian Churches experienced schism in the eleventh century (see Vol. 1, charts 130–34). The Western Church in turn was rent in the sixteenth century over questions concerning salvation, although the roots of this schism go back to the thirteenth century. The Protestant movement very soon gave birth to a number of Protestant groups, divided over doctrine and church government.

Chart 1

Views on Church Governance in the Protestant Reformation Teaching

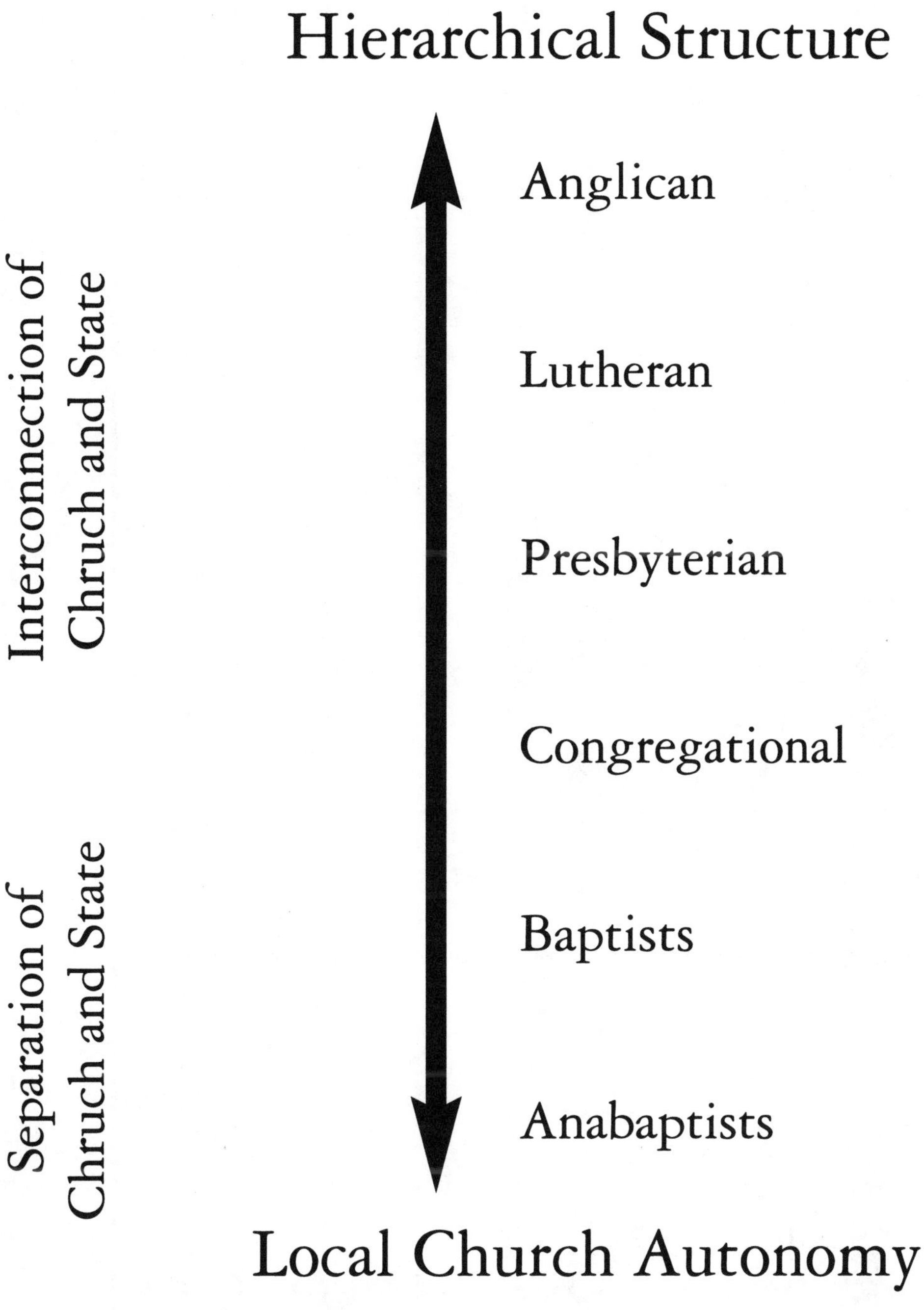

Hierarchical Structure

Interconnection of Chruch and State

Separation of Chruch and State

Anglican

Lutheran

Presbyterian

Congregational

Baptists

Anabaptists

Local Church Autonomy

As the Protestant movement distanced itself from the massively hierarchical structure of the Roman Catholic Church, with papal authority at its apex, it was not uniform in its understanding of church governance. Some Protestants developed hierarchical structures (Anglicanism), while churches in the Free Church tradition, such as the Anabaptists and Baptists, stressed local church autonomy. Thus Protestantism fragmented into Protestantisms.

Chart 2

The Three Fundamentals of
Protestant Reformation Teaching

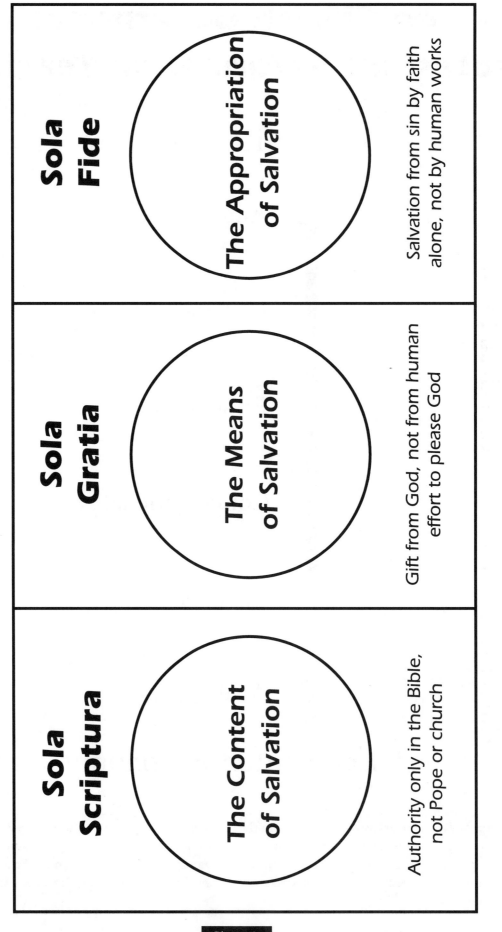

Sola Scriptura

The Content of Salvation

Authority only in the Bible, not Pope or church

Sola Gratia

The Means of Salvation

Gift from God, not from human effort to please God

Sola Fide

The Appropriation of Salvation

Salvation from sin by faith alone, not by human works

The essence of the Protestant Reformation has been summarized in three Latin phrases that together clearly state the essence of the gospel. Salvation is a gift from God, received through faith alone.

Chart 3

The Five "Solas" of the Protestant Reformation

	Sola Scriptura	Sola Christus	Sola Gratia	Sola Fide	Soli Deo Gloria
The Meaning:	Authority and Sufficiency of the Bible	Exclusivity of the Provider	Totality of Provision	Means of Appropriation	The Purpose of It All
Relative to Salvation:	Content	Basis	"Objective" (external) Cause	"Subjective" (personal) Agency	Reason for Living a Godly Life
It's Origin:	From God	From God's Son	From God's Pleasure	Through the Gift of Faith	For God's Glory

Chart 4

At some point the *solas* were expanded to five (we do not know by whom). Added were *Solus Christus* (or *Solo Christo*)—Christ alone is the procurer of salvation—and *Soli Deo* Gloria: God's glory is the purpose for which we now live.

Roman Catholic and Protestant Emphases in the Reformation

Justification by faith and sacraments → **Justification by faith alone**

Grace administered through church → **Priesthood of all believers**

Authority of Scripture and tradition → **Bible alone as final authority**

These three areas of difference between the Roman Catholic Church and the Protestant churches lie at the heart of the schism that took place in the sixteenth century. In each of these three areas the Roman Catholic Church assigns a key role to the church past and/or present, a role the Reformation churches reject.

Chart 5

Traditions within the Protestant Reformation

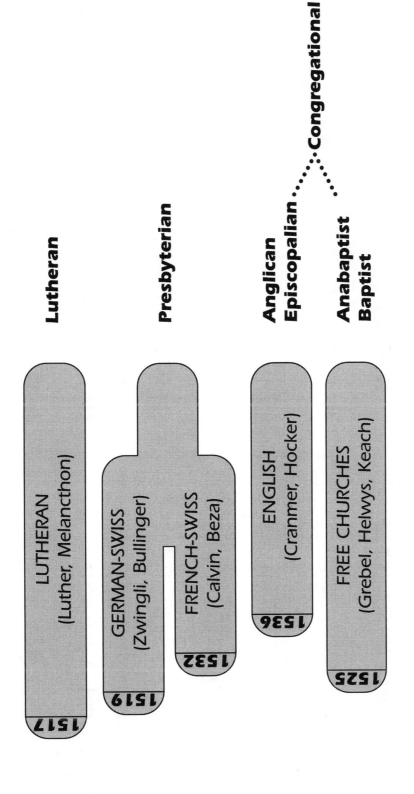

Lutheran

LUTHERAN
(Luther, Melancthon)
1517

Presbyterian

GERMAN-SWISS
(Zwingli, Bullinger)
1519

FRENCH-SWISS
(Calvin, Beza)
1532

Anglican
Episcopalian

Congregational

ENGLISH
(Cranmer, Hocker)
1536

Anabaptist
Baptist

FREE CHURCHES
(Grebel, Helwys, Keach)
1525

The Protestant Reformers differed among themselves on issues such as church government, the meaning of baptism and the Eucharist, and the relationship of the church to the state. These disagreements, as well as cultural and social differences, made unity impossible, and four major traditions emerged: the Lutheran, Calvinist (or Reformed), Anglican (or Church of England), and Free Church traditions.

Chart 6

Two Protestant Approaches to Reformation

MAGISTERIAL REFORMATION	RADICAL REFORMATION
Reform the Church	Reinstitute the Church
Gradual Change	Immediate Change
Endorse State Church	Reject State Church
Accept Concept of a Christian Magistrate (Political Authority)	Reject Concept of a Christian Magistrate (Political Authority)
Infant Baptism	Believer's Baptism

Among the reformers, two general approaches to church and cultural renewal are evident: magisterial reform (Lutheran, Presbyterian) and radical (or Free-Church) reform (Anabaptist). The former embraced the notion that effective reform could be carried out by cooperating with political structures. The Free Church traditions, called radical by the magisterial advocates, embraced a belief that the church should be composed of only professing believers and thus rejected infant baptism.

Chart 7

The Development of Church Government

Luther
Luther

Princes must safeguard the churches by having a say in pastoral appointments and maintaining orthodox teaching; the churches would have a measure of freedom to direct daily affairs.

Presbyterian and Reformed
Calvin

The locus of authority lies with the gathering of pastor and lay leaders called the session of the church. Matters that concerned the churches were to be determined in presbytery, a gathering of pastor and lay leaders from the churches in a given area.

Congregational
Anabaptist, Baptist

The authority for decision making rests with the members of each local church. Associations or conferences of churches and the decisions these bodies rendered are considered advisory only.

Episcopalian
Anglican (Church of England)

Authority rests with bishops and archbishops, but the notion of a single bishop over the church is rejected. The head of the church in England is the head of state.

Chart 8

Because the reformers were unified in rejecting papal hierarchical authority, they had to deal with the issue of what a biblical government of the church should look like. They did not agree.

The Relationship between Church and State

	ROMAN CATHOLIC	ANABAPTIST	CALVINIST	LUTHERAN
Kingdoms/	2	2	2	2
Authorities/	1	2	2	2
Allegiances	1	1	2	2
Relationship of State to Church	Subservient, unequal	Separate, unequal	Separate but equal	Separate but equal
Nature of the State	Divinely Ordained	Evil	Divinely Ordained but Evil	Evil
Duty of State to Church	State is an arm of the church State is authorized to impose faith	None	State is to assist in propagation of faith (religious responsibility) State is authorized to impose faith	State must maintain reason and order (secular responsibility) State is authorized to impose order
Basis for Change in Society	Faith	None	Faith	Reason
Participation in the State	Yes	No	Yes	Yes

Roman Catholics consistently held that the state was subservient to the church; Lutherans and Calvinists that the church and state operated in distinct and equal spheres under God; Anabaptists generally viewed the state with suspicion.

Chart 9

The Lutheran Reformation

The Development of Lutheranism

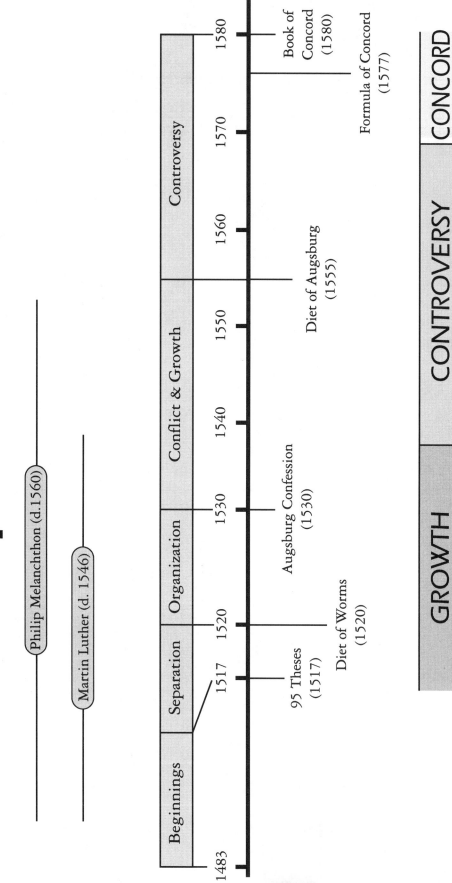

Philip Melanchthon (d.1560)

Martin Luther (d. 1546)

Beginnings	Separation	Organization	Conflict & Growth	Controversy
1483	1517 1520	1530	1540 1550	1560 1570 1580

95 Theses (1517)

Diet of Worms (1520)

Augsburg Confession (1530)

Diet of Augsburg (1555)

Formula of Concord (1577)

Book of Concord (1580)

GROWTH   CONTROVERSY   CONCORD

Chart 10

Era of beginnings: earliest years, education, admission to holy orders, and teaching at the university in Wittenberg; it ends with the events surrounding the Ninety-Five Theses. Era of separation: Luther's increasing hostility to the Roman Catholic Church, various debates and writings, ends with the confrontation with Charles V at Worms in 1521. Era of organization: shaping of the Lutheran movement, ending with the Augsburg Confession (1530). Era of conflict and growth: the struggles of the movement against the hostilities of the emperor; toleration granted at the Diet of Augsburg (1555). With Luther's death in 1546, Lutheranism became increasingly divided by theological debates from within.

The Luther Rose:
The Gospel in Symbol

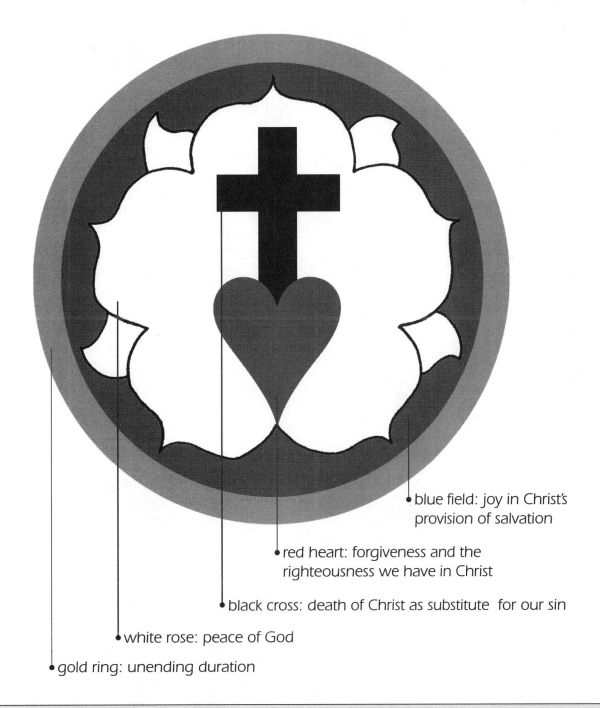

blue field: joy in Christ's provision of salvation

red heart: forgiveness and the righteousness we have in Christ

black cross: death of Christ as substitute for our sin

white rose: peace of God

gold ring: unending duration

Luther used the symbol of the rose (the so-called "Luther Rose") to convey the meaning of the gospel. At the center stands a red heart on which stands a black cross, conveying the cleansing of the heart through the substitutionary death of Christ on the cross. The heart is placed in a white rose within a blue field, encircled by a gold ring. This depicts the benefits of God's salvation. The white rose represents the peace of God through the blood of the cross, the blue field represents the experience of joy in Christ's provision of salvation, and the gold ring stands for its unending duration.

Chart 11

Stages in the Development of Luther's Concept of Justification

	1513		1518
Justification	Personal Justification	Analytic Justification	Personal Justification
Person of God	Punitive Judge	Enabler	Gracious Savior
Foundation of Forgiveness	Human Works	Christ's Work in Us (to make righteous)	Christ's Work in Us (to declare righteous)
Source of View	Scholastic Nominalism	Staupitz	The Bible (Romans 1:17)
View Held in	Pelagianism	Medieval Catholicism	Normative Protestantism

Chart 12

The central insight that Luther gained from the study of the Bible was that we are made right with God through the righteousness of Christ, not through our actions. This was a truth that Luther came to gradually understand.

The Calvinist Reformation

The Reformation in Switzerland

The History of the Swiss Reformations

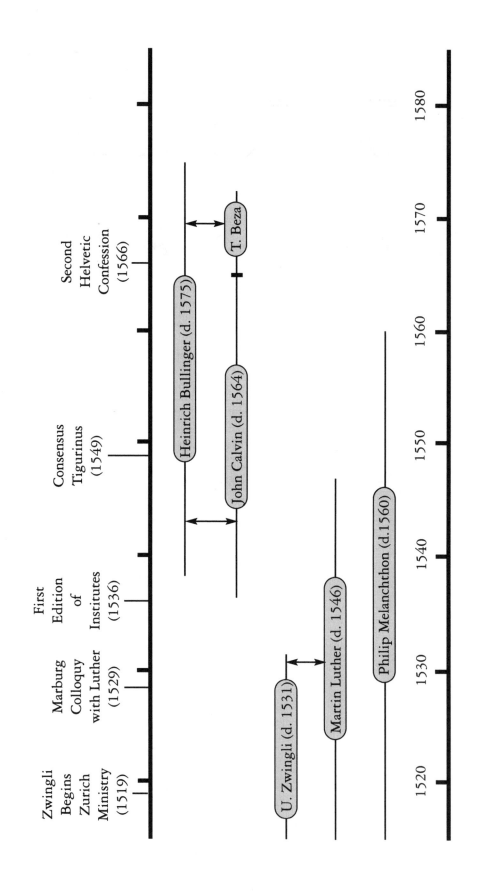

Zwingli Begins Zurich Ministry (1519)

Marburg Colloquy with Luther (1529)

First Edition of Institutes (1536)

Consensus Tigurinus (1549)

Second Helvetic Confession (1566)

1520　1530　1540　1550　1560　1570　1580

U. Zwingli (d. 1531)

Martin Luther (d. 1546)

Philip Melanchthon (d.1560)

John Calvin (d. 1564)

Heinrich Bullinger (d. 1575)

T. Beza

Chart 13

In Switzerland, Zwingli was the leader of the new reformation faith. After his death, two centers of Reformation emerged. Heinrich Bullinger succeeded Zwingli in Zurich; and in French-speaking Geneva, reformation ideas took root through William Farel and John Calvin. Calvin and his successor, Theodore Beza, were able to reach agreement with Bullinger in Zurich, and in 1566 the two Reformed movements merged around the Second Helvetic Confession. They had agreed earlier on the Eucharist (*Consensus Tigurinus*, 1549). Luther and Zwingli could not reach agreement at Marburg in 1529.

Theological Differences between the Lutheran and Calvinist Reformations

Issue	Lutheran Position	Reformed Position
Ordo Salutis	Calling, illumination, conversion, regeneration, justification, sanctification, glorification	Election, predestination, union with Christ, calling, regeneration, faith, repentance, justification, sanctification, glorification
Grace of God	Grace received through baptism or preaching enables one to avoid resisting the regenerating grace of God	Irresistible
Repentance	Leads to faith	Flows from faith
Baptism	Causes regeneration, removing guilt and power of sin	Incorporation into the Covenant of Grace
The Law	To reveal God's holiness and drive the sinner to Christ	To reveal God's holiness, to drive the sinner to Christ, and to show the believer how to please God (sanctification).
Lord's Supper	Christ present in the sacrament objectively	Sign and seal of the Covenant of Grace to believers; Christ present by faith
Church and State	The Church to tutor in the faith the rulers who support Protestantism	Holy Commonwealth in which church and state both Christian yet perform their separate functions
Regulative Principle	Whatever is not forbidden in Scripture is permissible	Whatever is not commanded in Scripture is forbidden

Though reformers across Europe found unity in Calvin's masterful *Institutes of the Christian Religion,* two distinct Protestant traditions emerged: Lutheran and Calvinist. Peace between the two was not possible because of theological differences and personal animosities.

Chart 14

The Great Eucharistic Divide

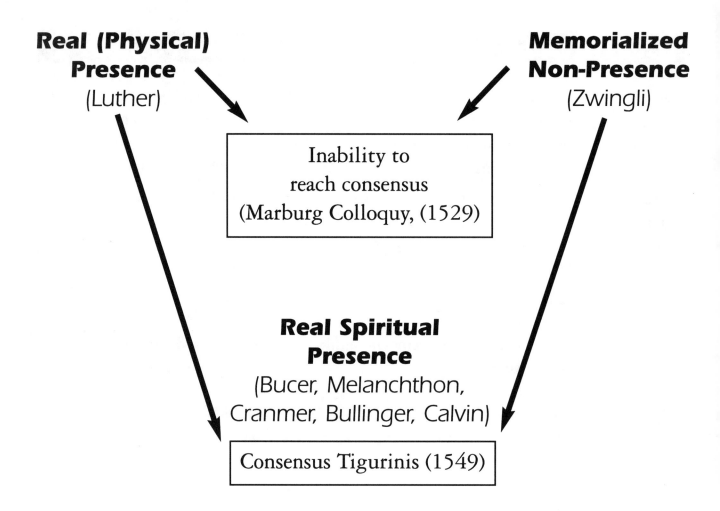

Real (Physical) Presence
(Luther)

Memorialized Non-Presence
(Zwingli)

Inability to
reach consensus
(Marburg Colloquy, (1529)

Real Spiritual Presence
(Bucer, Melanchthon, Cranmer, Bullinger, Calvin)

Consensus Tigurinis (1549)

The agreement at the Colloquy of Marburg in 1529 on fourteen articles of Protestant faith left little room for disagreement—except for the one remaining article on the Eucharist. After Luther's death a consensus was reached (the *Consensus Tigurinus,* 1549) between Bucer of Strassburg, Cranmer of England, Bullinger of Zurich, Calvin of Geneva, and Melanchthon of Wittenberg (Luther's conciliatory successor). On other issues, however, conciliatory Calvinists and Lutherans could not agree.

Chart 15

The Spread of Calvinism in Europe

The Reformation in Holland

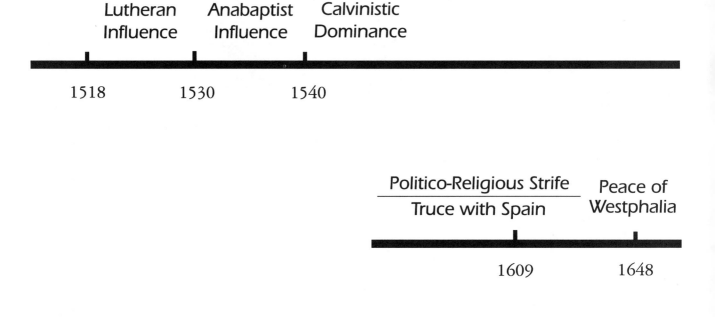

Lutheran Influence — 1518
Anabaptist Influence — 1530
Calvinistic Dominance — 1540

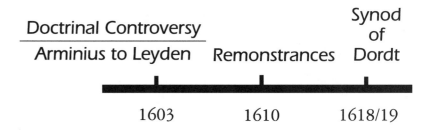

Politico-Religious Strife
Truce with Spain — 1609
Peace of Westphalia — 1648

Doctrinal Controversy
Arminius to Leyden — 1603
Remonstrances — 1610
Synod of Dordt — 1618/19

The faith of the emerging nation was Calvinistic, adopting the Belgic Confession (1561) and the Heidelberg Catechism (1562). Faced with an increasingly rationalistic spirit, some advocated changes in Calvinism as the best defense of the faith. Dirck Coornheert (1522–90) was openly critical of the Heidelberg Catechism and advocated leniency toward religious dissenters. Jacob Arminius believed that the best way to counter Coornheert was to modify Calvinist predestinarianism. In 1610, the year after Arminius' death, his followers presented their agenda for change, the *Five Remonstrances*. They were rebuffed at the Synod of Dordt (1618–19) and the "Remonstrants" were ostracized.

Chart 16

The Formation of Theology in the Reformation Era

	Roman Catholicism	Arminianism	Calvinism
	REACTION 16TH CENTURY →		**REACTION** 17TH CENTURY →
Salvation	Cooperation (Church, Man, and God)	Gracious Cooperation (God and Man)	Grace
Man	Moral and Spiritual Ability	Spiritual Ability	Moral and Spiritual Inability

As Calvinism was a sixteenth-century reaction against the errant teachings of the Roman Catholic Church, so Arminianism was a seventeenth-century movement that attempted to correct an overstated Calvinism. Two issues divided them: the mystery of the divine workings of God in salvation and the freedom of the human will.

Chart 17

Divine Sovereignty and Human Responsibility

Calvinists: A Mystery (both are true because God said so!) Redeeming grace limited in scope, not sufficiency. Divine security through assured perseverance.

Lutherans: Grace universal, effectual only for the elect. Redeeming grace unlimited in scope and sufficiency. Redeeming grace can be lost.

Arminians: Stress on responsibility, neglect of sovereignty. Redeeming grace unlimited in scope and sufficiency. Redeeming grace can be lost.

The major traditions in the Protestant Reformation grappled with the question of the relationship between human responsibility and divine sovereignty.

Chart 18

The Atonement in Calvinism and Arminianism

	CALVINISM	ARMINIANISM
The Meaning	Christ died for the sin of sinners. *A substitute penalty.*	Christ died for the sin principle. *A substitute for a penalty.*
The Purpose	To secure the foundation of forgiveness and righteousness.	To secure a disposition of possibility.
The Focus	To secure God's forgiveness and righteousness.	To allow God to make a plan to secure salvation.
The Result	Salvation	Salvability, the possibility for God to grant salvation upon certain conditions.

A central difference between Calvinists and Arminians was in the description of the death of Christ. The Calvinists hold that Christ died as a penal bearing substitute for selected sinners, completely paying their debt for sin and thereby satisfying the wrath of God toward them. The Arminians viewed Christ as dying on the cross for the idea of sin's penalty—a generic penalty for mankind. In seeking to preserve freedom, Arminians allowed contingency. Calvinists were unwilling to allow for contingency and so stressed divine finality.

Chart 19

Calvinism and Arminianism: A Comparison

Issue	Calvinist Position	Arminian Position
Ordo Salutis	Election, predestination, union with Christ, calling, regeneration, faith, repentance, justification, sanctification, glorification	Calling, faith, repentance, regeneration, justification, perseverance, glorification
Perseverance	Perseverance of all the elect by the grace of God	Perseverance dependent on obedience
Atonement	Christ's death a substitutionary penal sacrifice	Christ's death a sacrifice that God benevolently accepted in place of a penalty
Extent of Atonement	Intended only for the elect	Intended for all
Application of Atonement	By power of the Holy Spirit according to the will of God	By power of the Holy Spirit in response to the will of the sinner
Original Sin	Total depravity and guilt inherited from Adam	Weakness inherited from Adam
Human Will	In bondage to sin	Free to do spiritual good if willing
Grace of God	Common grace given to all; saving grace given to elect	Enabling grace given to all; saving grace given to those who believe; persevering grace given to those who obey
Predestination	Rooted in God's decrees	Rooted in God's foresight
Regeneration	Monergistic	Synergistic

Chart 20

Calvinists consistently attempted to see God's dealings with mankind from an eternal perspective; Arminians focused more on human freedom. At the heart of the debate were differing views on the inheritance of disability through Adam. Calvinists traditionally view the effects as much more devastating than Arminians do, thereby stressing divine choice rather than human initiative. Arminians believe that God's determinations were based on what he foresaw of mankind's response to grace; Calvinists felt that such a view of causation denied the sovereignty of God.

The Five Points of Calvinism

T   Total Depravity
Due to Adam's sin, man's human nature is corrupt, and every person stands condemned in God's sight. If God does not act directly on an individual, that person has no hope of ever being saved.

U   Unconditional Election
God elects certain persons to be saved, based solely upon his determination, utterly apart from anything a person may or may not do.

L   Limited Atonement
The atonement is limited in that Christ died only for the elect.

I   Irresistible Grace
God' election also involves His acting in grace on the elect toward their salvation; they cannot resist the power of His Spirit to save.

P   Perseverance of the Saints
Once someone has been saved by God, they remain forever in that condition. They will persevere until the very end of their lives.

When the Arminian or Remonstrant Party petitioned the National Church to revise its creedal standards, they did so with the presentation of a document called the *Five Remonstrants*. The Calvinist Party responded several years later at Dordt with an affirmation of their own, condemning the Remonstrants and correcting its errors. Calvinists responded with what has become known as the "Five Points of Calvinism," though the documents issued from Dordt contains only four articles.

Chart 21

The Progression of the Reformation in France

1515–1547
Francis I

1559–1560
Charles IX
(married Mary Queen of Scots)

1575–1589
Henry III

1594–1610

| Periods of Beginnings | Period under Calvin | Period of Religious War | Period of Toleration |

1512

1536

1560

1598

1685

1512 "The beginnings of the Protestant movement in France, with the publication of a commentary on Paul's epistles by Jacques Faber (Lefevre; c. 1455–1536).

1536 Calvin's Institutes are first published; the work is dedicated to King Francis I of France (1515–47).

1547–1559
Henry II

1559 The Protestant movement flourishes so that in 1559 at the Synod of Paris the French Protestant church is formed with some two thousand churches.

1560 Beginning of almost four decades of religio-political strife, epitomized by the infamous St. Bartholomew massacre of Protestants (1572).

1560-1574
Charles IX

1598 Henry of Navarre becomes king and grants Protestantism religious freedom by issuing the Edict of Nantes.

1685 Louis XIV revokes the edict of Nantes; Protestants (Huguenots) flee France by the tens of thousands across Europe and into the New World.

Chart 22

The Reformation in Scotland

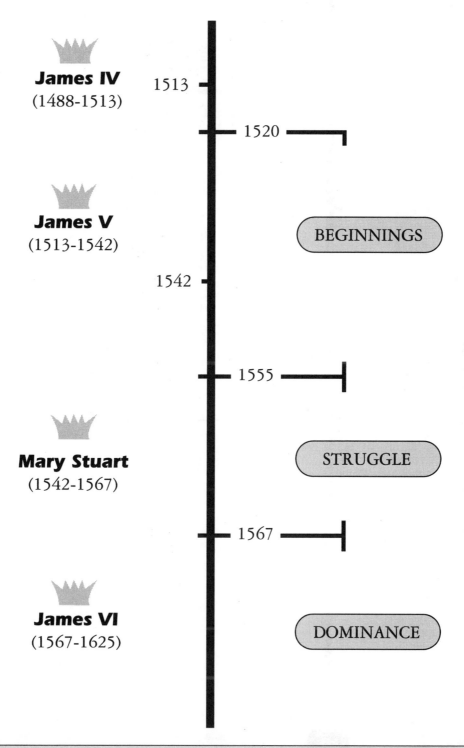

James IV
(1488-1513)

1513

1520

James V
(1513-1542)

BEGINNINGS

1542

1555

Mary Stuart
(1542-1567)

STRUGGLE

1567

James VI
(1567-1625)

DOMINANCE

The earliest Protestant influences in Scotland were Lutheran; in 1528 Patrick Hamilton was martyred at St. Andrews for advocating Lutheran principles. The leadership of the emerging Protestant movement then fell to John Knox. As a later exile in England, Knox was forced to flee to Europe where he became a disciple of Calvin in Geneva. In 1555 he returned to Scotland to become the vocal leader of the Protestant movement. The reformed Protestant Church of Scotland was formed in 1560. With the abdication of Mary Queen of Scots in 1567 and the ascension of her son, James VI, Protestantism flourished.

Chart 23

The History of the Church of Scotland (Covenanters)

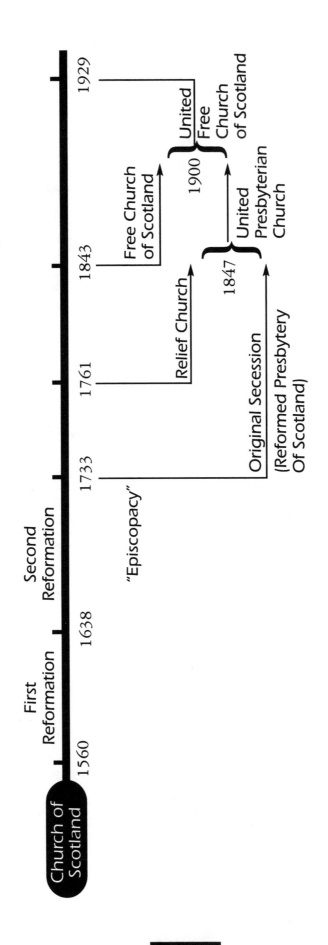

Beginning about 1560, the Scots struggled to establish a national Protestant church, free of Roman Catholic doctrine and control. Almost a century later they struggled against the imposition of Anglicanism on the Scottish Church through William Laud, the archbishop of Canterbury under Charles II. This struggle is viewed as the "Second Reformation." The Scots signed the National Covenant in 1638, pledging their all for their church, and thus became "Covenanters." The Church of Scotland suffered a number of schisms and mergers over the centuries that followed.

Chart 24

The Anabaptist Reformation

Varieties within the Anabaptist Tradition (The Radical Reformation)

Orthodox

Conservative in their views. They advocated pacifism, usually following the unique insights of a leader such as Jacob Hutter or Menno Simons. In Switzerland they were former followers of Zwingli and were known as Swiss Brethren.

Spiritualists

Known as Schwenkenfelders. These Anabaptists stressed the inner leading of the Spirit, thereby denigrating the unity of the Spirit of God and the Word of God.

Rationalists

These Anabaptists injected a rationalistic spirit into Christianity and denied such fundamental doctrines as the trinity of God, the deity of Christ, and blood atonement. Such views were those of Michael Servetus (1511–53) and the Socinians.

Radicals

They adopted a strong antiestablishmentarian stance. Centered in Zwickau, hence known as the Zwickau Prophets.

The Anabaptist tradition includes a spectrum of beliefs and practices (in fact, some Baptists reject any Continental origins for their movement to avoid guilt-by-association). Scholars have preferred to gather them together under the title "The Radical Reformation." Although there is a wide variety of theologies in the Radical Tradition, there is consensus on the notion of separation of church and state, an affirmation of believers' baptism, and a stress on the gathered church.

Chart 25

Four Views on Baptist Beginnings

Continental Origins

Understanding of Baptist roots developed thus far is called the Continental Origins view. It finds the origin of the Baptist movement in the Reformation in Zurich that spread throughout Europe, particularly Holland, and to England where the Baptist tradition as we know it today is founded.

Silver Line of Grace

A view developed in England in the eighteenth, and in America in the nineteenth century is what is known as "the trail of Blood," "the silver line of grace," or "Landmarkism." According to this view Baptists are not Protestants. They can trace their origins from the birth of the church down through the centuries in a succession of "Baptist" churches.

English Separatist Origins (I)

This view sees Baptist origins as rooted in the English Reformation of the seventeenth century, particularly in the Puritan movement that embraced Calvinism in theology and repudiated Anglican sacramentalism in worship. According to one variant of this view, some English separatists fled to Holland to escape persecution and embraced Mennonite views. Returning to England in 1612, they established the General Baptist movement.

English Separatist Origins (II)

More likely, Baptist beginnings are found among those who rejected Anglicanism and Presbyterianism for a Congregational understanding of church government, then adding the notion of believers baptism. The Puritan Congregationalists-turned-Baptists emerged in the 1640s adopting the Particular Baptist Confession of 1644 as its doctrinal standard.

Chart 26

History of the English Baptists

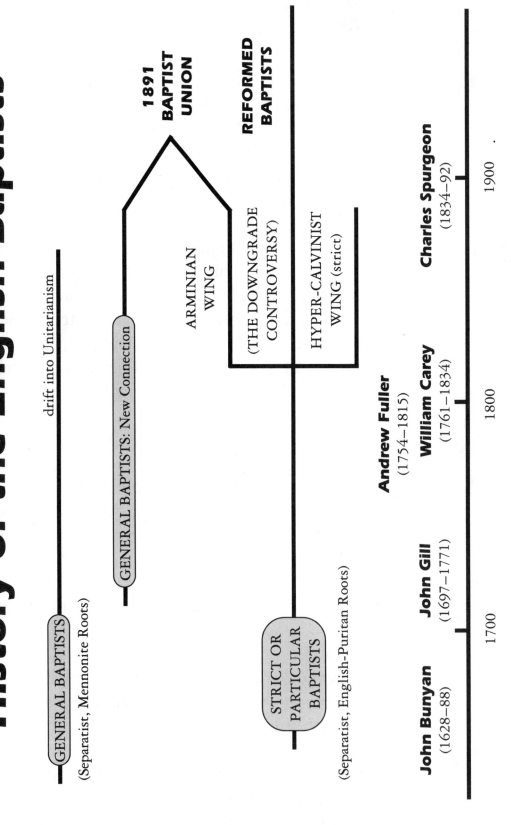

GENERAL BAPTISTS
(Separatist, Mennonite Roots)

drift into Unitarianism

GENERAL BAPTISTS: New Connection

1891 BAPTIST UNION

ARMINIAN WING

REFORMED BAPTISTS

(THE DOWNGRADE CONTROVERSY)

HYPER-CALVINIST WING (strict)

STRICT OR PARTICULAR BAPTISTS

(Separatist, English-Puritan Roots)

John Bunyan
(1628–88)

John Gill
(1697–1771)

Andrew Fuller
(1754–1815)

William Carey
(1761–1834)

Charles Spurgeon
(1834–92)

1700

1800

1900

The General Baptists have English separatist roots and Mennonite influence from their brief stay in Holland. They returned to England in 1612 and gradually drifted into Unitarianism. Strict or Particular Baptists came from English Puritan Congregationalism in the 1640s. This Baptist group split in the late 1800s. Later, some of the General Baptist heritage merged with the least Calvinistic segment of the Particular Baptists in the Baptist Union of 1891. Some great names are associated with the Strict or Reformed Baptists: John Bunyan; the theologian John Gill; the missionary William Carey; and the great preacher/soul-winner, Charles Spurgeon.

Chart 27

The English Reformation

The Protestant Reformations on the Continent and in England

"On the Continent, the Reformation began with religion and ended in politics."	"In England, the Reformation began with politics and ended in religion."
Martin Luther *Ninety-Five Theses*	Henry VIII *Six Wives* 1. Catherine of Aragon (⟶ Mary) 2. Anne Boleyn (⟶ Elizabeth) 3. Jane Seymour (⟶ Edward) 4. Anne of Cleves 5. Catherine Howard 6. Catherine Parr

Henry VIII sought from the church an annulment of his marriage to Catherine of Aragon in order to marry another, who happened to be in the late stages of pregnancy. The request was denied, so Henry turned to parliament. The Church of England was born with the British monarch rather than the Pope at its head. Thus the roots of the tolerance of Protestant views in England lie with the clash between Henry VIII and the papacy.

Chart 28

The Reformation and the English Monarchs

Date	Monarch	Church
1509	Henry VIII	Reformed Catholicism
1547	Edward VI	Advanced Protestantism
1553	Mary Tudor	Militant Catholicism
1558	Elizabeth I	Episcopalianism
1603	James I	Enforced Episcopalianism
1625	Charles I	
1640	Presbyterian	Transcendent Puritanism
1649	Independent	
1660	Charles II	Enforced Episcopalianism
1685	James II	
1689	William III	Religious Toleration

THE TUDOR MONARCHS

THE STUART MONARCHS

THE HOUSE OF ORANGE

RISE OF PURITANISM

Chart 29

Henry VIII separated the church from the papacy, making himself its head. Under his successor, Calvinist Protestantism defined the church through the creation of the Prayer Books by Archbishop Thomas Cranmer. Queen Mary reestablished Roman Catholicism, while Elizabeth I sought to create a church that would be poignantly neither Roman nor Protestant. The Puritans gained ascendancy in the 1640s and sought to reform the church, without success. The monarchy was dissolved and the king and archbishop killed. The monarchy was restored in 1660 and the Puritan movement suppressed. Religious strife blended into toleration with the ascension of William III in 1688.

Religious Shifts in the English Reformation

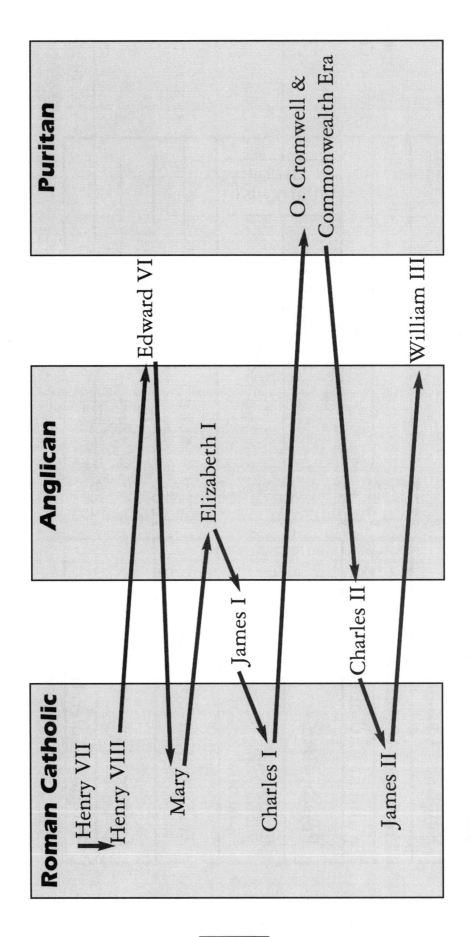

Roman Catholic	Anglican	Puritan
Henry VII		
Henry VIII		
	Edward VI	
Mary		
	Elizabeth I	
James I		
Charles I		
		O. Cromwell & Commonwealth Era
Charles II		
James II		
	William III	

This diagram complements the preceding chart. It shows graphically how the religious faith or preferences of the monarchs of England had an impact on the English church.

Chart 30

The Rise of Puritanism in Elizabethan England

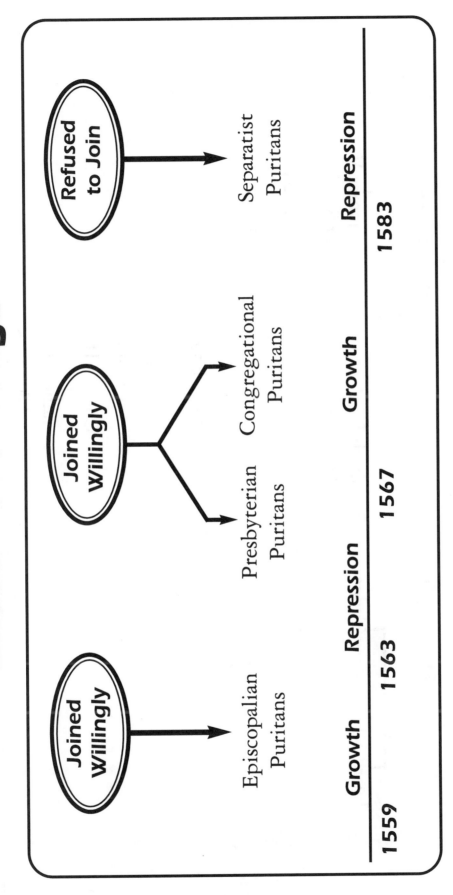

Joined Willingly	Joined Willingly	Refused to Join
Episcopalian Puritans	Presbyterian Puritans / Congregational Puritans	Separatist Puritans

Growth	Repression	Growth	Repression
1559	1563	1567	1583

Chart 31

The reign of Elizabeth I witnessed the establishment of the Church of England as the Episcopal or Anglican community. It was a church defined by Elizabeth's discomfort with Roman Catholicism and Protestantism. The church adopted a Lutheran willingness to affirm a measure of political headship over the church, liturgical ritual in worship, and a mild Calvinism in theology. This troubled many, particularly those who had been influenced by Calvinism with its emphasis on simplicity in worship style. A movement gradually emerged in England as an alternative to Episcopalianism: Puritanism. This movement was suppressed during the reign of Elizabeth.

The Emergence of the Stuart Dynasty of Scotland to the English Monarchy

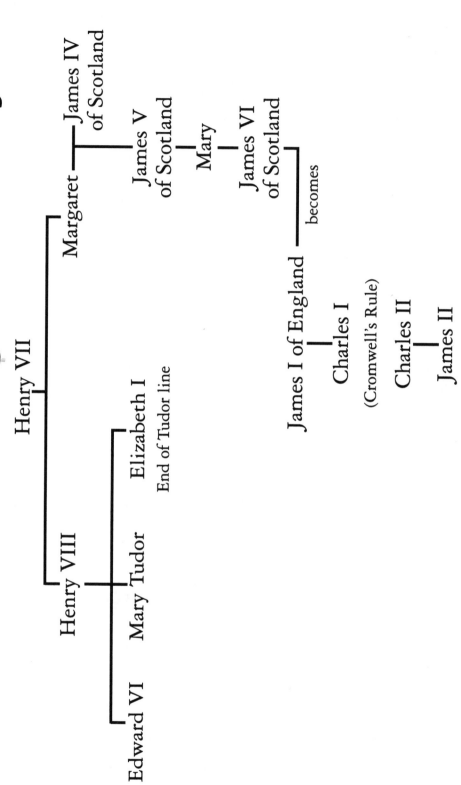

Henry VII

Margaret —— James IV
of Scotland

Henry VIII

James V
of Scotland

Mary

James VI
of Scotland

becomes

Edward VI   Mary Tudor   Elizabeth I
                           End of Tudor line

James I of England

Charles I

(Cromwell's Rule)

Charles II

James II
End of Stuart line

Two dynasties span the era of the Protestant Reformation in English history: the Tudors of the sixteenth century and the Stuarts of the seventeenth. The death of Elizabeth I in 1603 brought an end to the Tudor line, since she had no children. The throne of England passed to the king of Scotland because Henry VIII's sister had married James IV. James VI became James I of England in 1603. The Stuart line ended with the abdication of James II and the ascension of William III of Holland to the throne in 1688.

Chart 32

The Rise of English Presbyterianism

Emergence of Presbyterian Puritanism

1558	1563	1570	1572
Elizabethan Settlement	Vestments Controversy	Cartwright's Lecture on Acts	Admonitions Controversy

Triumph of Presbyterian Puritanism

1584	1643-8
Disciplina Ecclesiae	Westminster Assembly of Divines

Westminster Assembly of Divines →
1. Directory of Church Government
2. Westminster Confession
3. Larger Catechism
4. Shorter Catechism

Presbyterianism in England is rooted in the Elizabethan Settlement of 1558, which established the Church of England as an Episcopal community. Reaction to the establishment of Episcopalianism was evident in the Vestments Controversy, concerning the wearing of certain clerical garments, and the Admonitions Controversy (1572), a plea to parliament to rid the church of popery. Thomas Cartwright's lectures on the book of Acts at Cambridge as well as his influence on the earliest statement of church government, the *Disciplina Ecclesiae*, laid the foundation for the work of the Westminster Assembly.

Chart 33

Nonconformity in England

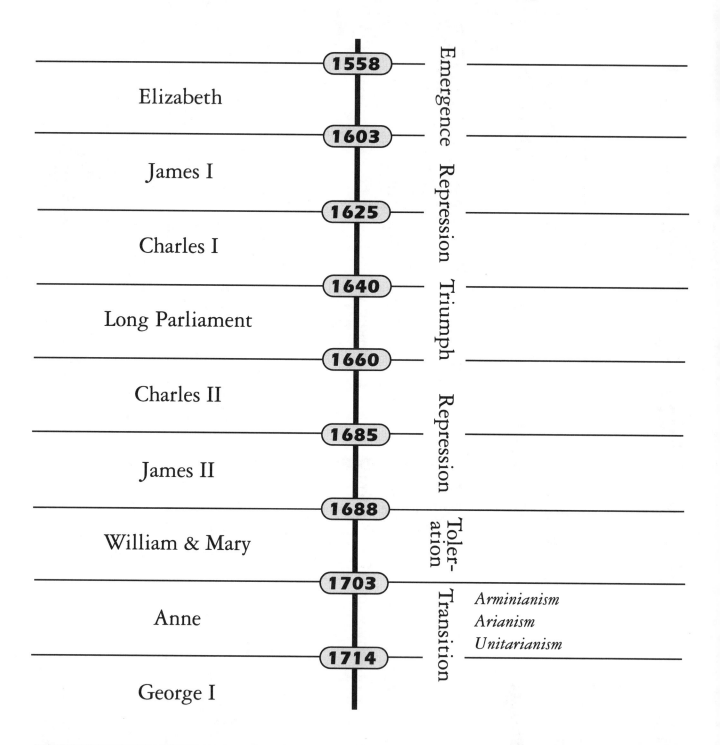

Monarch/Period	Year	Phase
	1558	Emergence
Elizabeth		
	1603	
James I		Repression
	1625	
Charles I		
	1640	Triumph
Long Parliament		
	1660	
Charles II		Repression
	1685	
James II		
	1688	Toleration
William & Mary		
	1703	Transition
Anne		*Arminianism*
		Arianism
		Unitarianism
	1714	
George I		

Various "nonconformist" alternatives to Episcopal rule struggled to emerge in the Elizabethan era and were repressed in the reigns of James I and Charles I. The religious and political oppression brought about civil war in the early 1640s, ending the monarchy and making nonconformism acceptable. With the restoration of the monarchy in 1660 all forms of nonepiscopacy were repressed in the 1660s and 70s: Baptists, Congregationalists, and Presbyterians felt the sting of the Clarendon Codes. Toleration came to Protestants of all stripes in England with the ascension of William III.

Chart 34

The English Bible in the Sixteenth Century

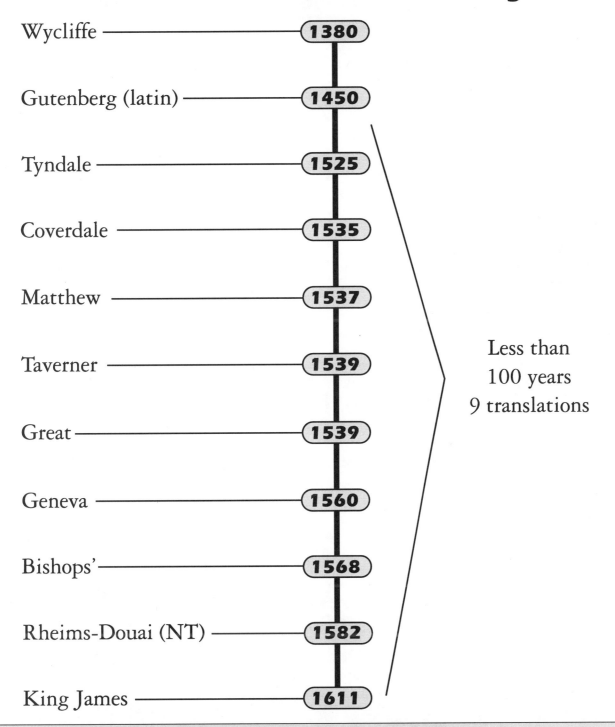

Wycliffe	1380	
Gutenberg (latin)	1450	
Tyndale	1525	Less than
Coverdale	1535	100 years
Matthew	1537	9 translations
Taverner	1539	
Great	1539	
Geneva	1560	
Bishops'	1568	
Rheims-Douai (NT)	1582	
King James	1611	

The era of the Reformation saw a flurry of translations of the Scriptures. The first complete Bible in English is commonly attributed to John Wycliffe, though we now know that it was the work of two of his disciples, Nicholas of Hereford and John Purvey. The advent of printing, exemplified in the famous Gutenberg Bible, had an enormous effect on the availability of Bible knowledge. The first printed Bible in English, and the first done independently of the Latin Vulgate (the Bible of the Medieval Era), was the work of William Tyndale.

Chart 35

The Roman Catholic Reformation ("Counter Reformation")

The History of the Roman Catholic Church: The Council of Trent

Trent
1545–63 ———————————— "We were hated"

Vatican I
1870 ———————————— "We were ignored"

Vatican II
1963–65 ———————————— "We were welcomed as errant brethren"

The creedal formulation of Roman Catholicism became most clearly articulated in the sixteenth century as the Late Medieval Church, having experienced religious decline, was reformed. In a formal council the Roman Catholic Church elucidated its doctrinal opinions in continuity with the centuries but, more importantly, in contrast to the Protestants. That grand defining council was held at Trent in Northern Italy. Two major councils would follow through the centuries, each with a different attitude toward their antagonists.

Chart 36

The Differences between Roman Catholicism and Protestantism

5 key Areas	PROTESTANT	ROMAN CATHOLIC
SCRIPTURE		
Sufficiency	• *Sola Scriptura*	• tradition of equal authority with Scripture
Apocrypha	• rejected	• accepted
ANTHROPOLOGY		
Original Sin	• total depravity & guilt inherited from Adam	• corruption and predisposition to do evil inherited from Adam
Human Will	• in bondage to sin	• free to do spiritual good
SOTERIOLOGY		
Good Works	• produced by the grace of God, unworthy of merit of any kind	• meritorious
Regeneration	• a work of the Holy Spirit in the elect	• grace infused at baptism, increase by sacrament
Justification	• an objective, final, judicial act of God	• forgiveness of sins received at baptism, may be lost by committing sin, regained by penance
Predestination Atonement	• rooted in God's decrees • Christ's death a substitutionary penal sacrifice	• rooted in God's foreknowledge Christ's death the merit for blessings of salvation—blessings passed on to sinners through sacraments
Grace of God	• common grace given to all; saving grace given to elect	• prevenient grace, given at baptism, enabling one to believe; efficacious grace cooperating with the will, enabling one to obey
ECCLESIOLOGY		
Church & Salvation	• distinction between visible and invisible church	• outside the (visible) church there is no salvation
Sacraments	• a means of grace only as received by faith	• conveys justifying and sanctifying grace *ex opere operato* (by works).
Priesthood	• all believers are priests	• priestly office mediates between God and man
Transubstantiation	• rejected	• affirmed
ESCHATOLOGY		
Purgatory	• denied	• affirmed

The confessions and creeds of the Protestants and Roman Catholics defined their differences.

Chart 37

Justification and the Council of Trent

Canon XXX

If any one saith, that, after the grace of Justification has been received, to every penitent sinner the guilt is remitted, and the debt of eternal punishment is blotted out in such wise that there remains not any debt of temporal punishment to be discharged either in this world, or in the next in Purgatory, before the entrance to the kingdom of heaven can be opened [to him]: let him be anathema.

Canon XXXII

If any one saith, that the good works of one that is justified are in such manner the gifts of God, that they are not also the good merits of him that is justified; or, that the said justified, by the good works which he performs through the grace of God and the merit of Jesus Christ, whose living member he is, does not truly merit increase of grace, eternal life, and the attainment of that eternal life,—if so be, however, that he depart in grace,—and also an increase of glory: let him be anathema.

The doctrine of Justification was one of the central issues that divided Roman Catholic and Protestant factions. It is not surprising that the Council of Trent made it a focus of discussion, both in several positive statements and in contrasting negative statements. The "anathema" sections were devised to specifically condemn the teachings of the Protestants. Canon XXX condemns the Protestant assertion that through grace alone, neither with the aid of sacrament, priest, or church, is one justified forever before a holy God. Canon XXXII condemned the Protestant interpretation of the role of works in justification.

Chart 38

THE RISE OF RELIGIOUS RATIONALISM AND THE ENLIGHTENMENT
(1650 to 1750)

Orthodoxy and Unitarianism Compared

	ORTHODOXY	UNITARIANISM
Source of Truth:	Reformation Empiricism Rationalism	Empiricism Rationalism Reformation
God:	Theistic; plural, personal	Theistic; single, personal
Medium of Revelation:	Supernatural, Natural	Natural, Supernatural
Person of Christ:	God/Man	Archetypal Man
Nature of Sin:	Derived and personal depravity; Moral inability	Personal depravity; Moral ability
Atonement:	Penal	Exemplary

Chart 39

Unitarians place rational ability and the scientific method above the Scriptures. They do not see a discontinuity between the supernatural truth of the Bible and common knowledge. God is single in person as well as in characteristics. Christ is simply the best of humankind and his death an inspiring moral example. The root of the Unitarian error is a rejection of the supernatural claims of the Bible and an unwillingness to believe in the dark side of the human condition.

Orthodoxy and Deism Compared

	ORTHODOXY	DEISM
Epistemology:	Reformation Empiricism Rationalism	Empiricism Rationalism
God:	Theistic; plural, personal	Theistic; single, utterly transcendent
Medium of Revelation:	Supernatural, Natural	Natural
Person of Christ:	God/Man	Exemplary Man
Nature of Sin:	Derived and personal depravity; Moral inability	Personal depravity; Moral ability
Atonement:	Penal	(none)

Chart 40

Deists share many of the religious ideas of the Unitarians, since both are expressions of theological Enlightenment rationalism. Unitarians tend to see God as personal and some of the miracles of the Bible as actually happening. Deists, on the other hand, see God as the Grand Creator who, like a clock-maker, simply watches the universe tick away and works through natural law alone, which makes miracles impossible. This distinction can be seen in the religious views of the Deist Benjamin Franklin and the Unitarian Thomas Jefferson.

THE ENLIGHTENMENT
(1650 to 1750)

Approaches to Authority and the Enlightenment

	Reformation 16th century		Enlightenment 18th century
	Roman Catholicism	**Protestantism**	**Rationalism**
authority	HOLY CHURCH → Authoritarianism Pope and councils	HOLY BIBLE → Creeds (Secondary)	HUMAN REASON → Philosophical Systems
salvation	GOD ⇄ CHURCH ⇄ MAN	GOD → CHRIST → MAN	GOD ← MAN

Chart 41

Enlightenment refers to a many-faceted movement in eighteenth-century western Europe that at its core rejected the Orthodox understanding of the sinfulness of mankind and the need for redemption through Jesus Christ. It is rooted in the negative features of the Renaissance of the fifteenth century and it emerged after the reformations of the Medieval Church in the sixteenth and seventeenth centuries. Two issues separated Roman Catholics and Protestants from Enlightenment advocates: the locus of authority, which the Enlightenment places in human reason, and the nature of salvation, which the Enlightenment seeks in human ingenuity and moral resolve. Roman Catholics and Protestants agreed that authority was not within, but outside of mankind. The former invested in religious knowledge mediated by the church; the latter in the Bible explained by pastors.

From Revelation to Reason

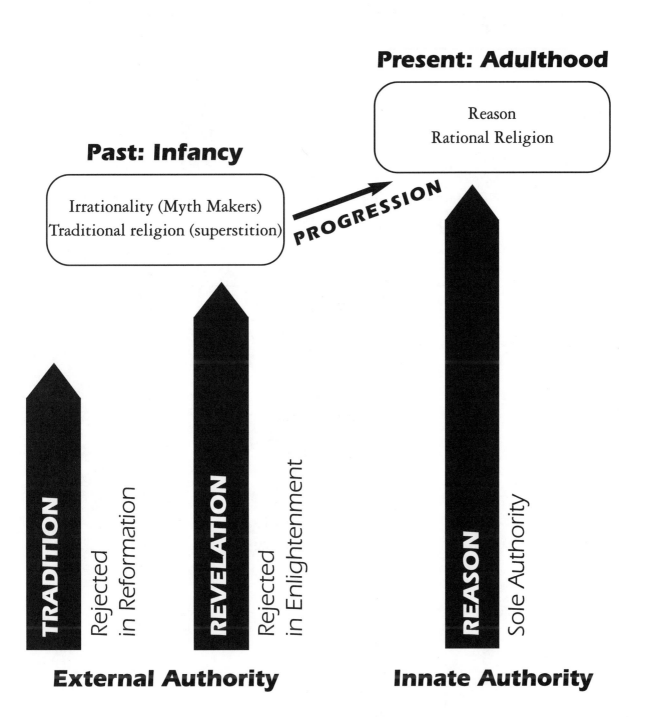

Present: Adulthood

Reason
Rational Religion

Past: Infancy

Irrationality (Myth Makers)
Traditional religion (superstition)

PROGRESSION

TRADITION — Rejected in Reformation

REVELATION — Rejected in Enlightenment

REASON — Sole Authority

External Authority

Innate Authority

Tradition was rejected as a source of authority in the Reformation. The other external source of authority, revelation, was rejected in the Enlightenment, leaving reason as the sole authority. The Enlightenment brought about a new, positive understanding of humanity and human capacities. External authority (such as religion) kept people in bondage and made it impossible for them to reach their fullest potential—to mature into self-trust and fulfillment, as is now possible through a more rational understanding of religious faith. Anything supernatural, such as miracles or the Incarnation and Resurrection, were the result of unconscious misperception or, worse, deliberate deception.

Chart 42

The Enlightenment and Knowledge

CARTESIANS
Rene Descartes
1596–1650

INNATE IDEAS / DOUBT

- God and nature give ideas

- We use rational reflection to understand

LOCKEANS
John Locke
1632–1704

EMPIRICISM

- "Tabula rasa": people begin with blank minds

- Experience of the senses gives ideas and understanding

KANTIANS
Immanuel Kant
1724–1804

INNATE IDEAS AND EMPIRICISM

- Humans cannot know God or the soul

- Spiritual and natural knowledge combine to create conscience, which is the starting place for religion because humans have moral sense

- We develop inherent morality through reason

- No revelation of God in the Bible is necessary; truth is based on experience

Descartes believed that human knowledge begins with doubt of everything except our ability to think, and that only through our reasoning can we know the existence of God. John Locke argued that knowledge comes from reflection on sense experience. Kant refined Descartes' and Locke's views, saying that knowledge falls into two categories: spiritual and physical. We cannot really know the spiritual, but through knowledge derived from the physical realm we order and understand our inherent spiritual morality. Deism is an outflow of these ideas.

Chart 43

The Roots of Modernity and Postmodernity

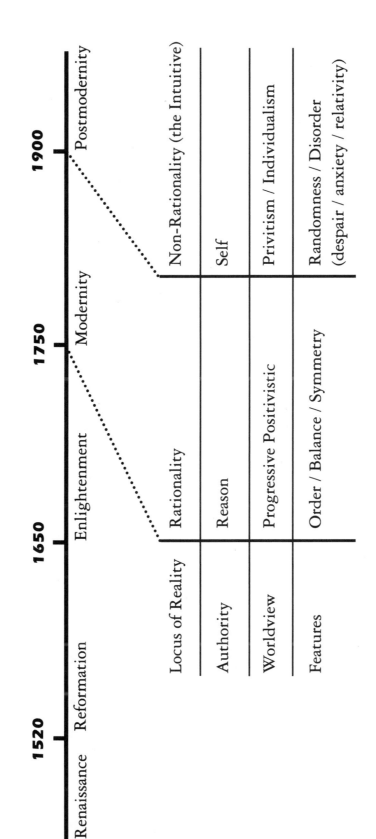

	1520	1650	1750	1900
	Renaissance	Reformation	Enlightenment	Modernity	Postmodernity

Locus of Reality	Rationality	Non-Rationality (the Intuitive)
Authority	Reason	Self
Worldview	Progressive Positivistic	Privitism / Individualism
Features	Order / Balance / Symmetry	Randomness / Disorder (despair / anxiety / relativity)

The Enlightenment provided the assumptions that undergirded the late Modern Era (1750–1900), which was characterized by an emphasis on the authority of reason and the virtues of education, a deep-seated optimism and commitment to an upward spiral of human improvability, and an attempt to define religion as improved morals. When the assumptions that undergirded the late Modern Era collapsed in the twentieth century, there was little to replace it except an even more radical emphasis on individualism, which has lead to societal despair, meaninglessness, and relativity.

Chart 44

The Reaction against Creedalism and Rationalism: Pietism

The Spread of Evangelical Pietism

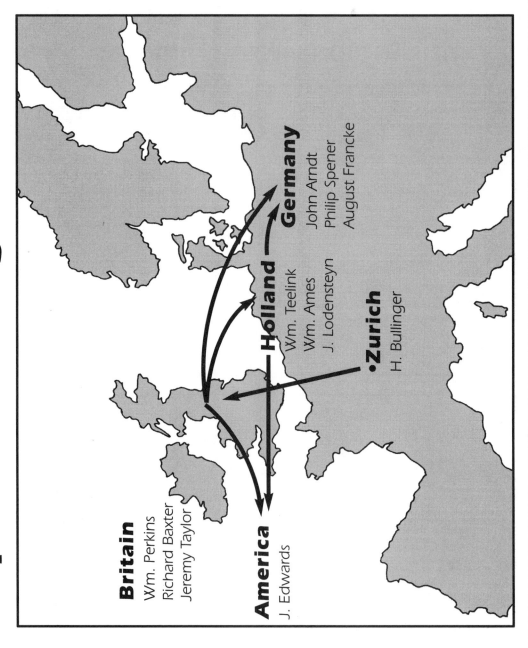

Britain
Wm. Perkins
Richard Baxter
Jeremy Taylor

Holland
Wm. Teelink
Wm. Ames
J. Lodensteyn

Germany
John Arndt
Philip Spener
August Francke

•**Zurich**
H. Bullinger

America
J. Edwards

Pietism was a movement in seventeenth-century Germany that was a reaction to creedal and rationalistic trends in the Lutheran Churches. With an emphasis of heart-felt faith and commitment, as well as Protestant orthodox faith, the roots of the movement may be traced to the English-man John Hooper, who had been impacted by the piety of the Zurich reformers. From England the movement emerged in Holland, Germany, and America.

Chart 45

The Origins of German Lutheran Pietism

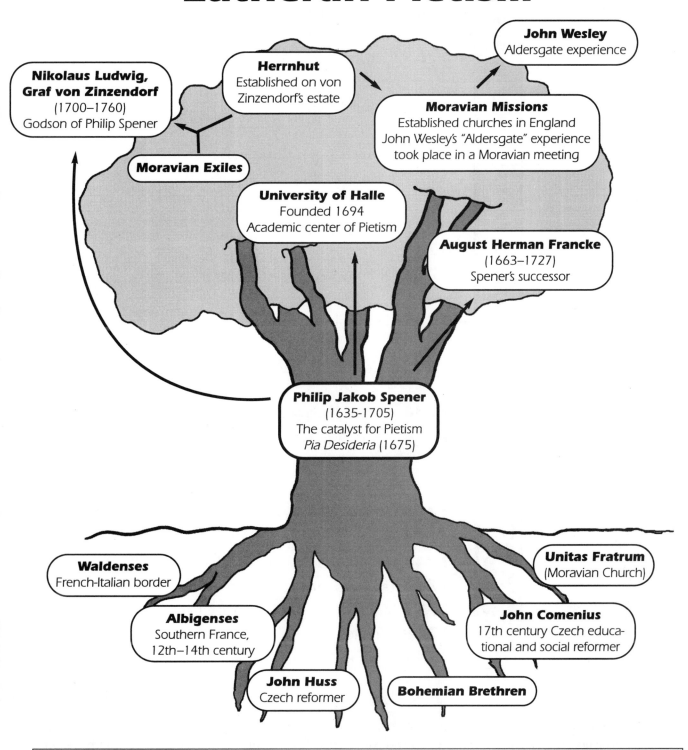

John Wesley
Aldersgate experience

Nikolaus Ludwig, Graf von Zinzendorf
(1700–1760)
Godson of Philip Spener

Herrnhut
Established on von Zinzendorf's estate

Moravian Missions
Established churches in England
John Wesley's "Aldersgate" experience took place in a Moravian meeting

Moravian Exiles

University of Halle
Founded 1694
Academic center of Pietism

August Herman Francke
(1663–1727)
Spener's successor

Philip Jakob Spener
(1635-1705)
The catalyst for Pietism
Pia Desideria (1675)

Waldenses
French-Italian border

Unitas Fratrum
(Moravian Church)

Albigenses
Southern France,
12th–14th century

John Comenius
17th century Czech educational and social reformer

John Huss
Czech reformer

Bohemian Brethren

The German Pietist Movement of the seventeenth century had many spiritual antecedents in Late Medievalism. Philip Spener's *Pious Desires* proved to be the catalyst for the movement that established its academic center at the University of Halle. There is a direct link between German Pietism and English Methodism; John Wesley had his life-changing experience at a Moravian meeting in London.

Chart 46

The Life of John Wesley

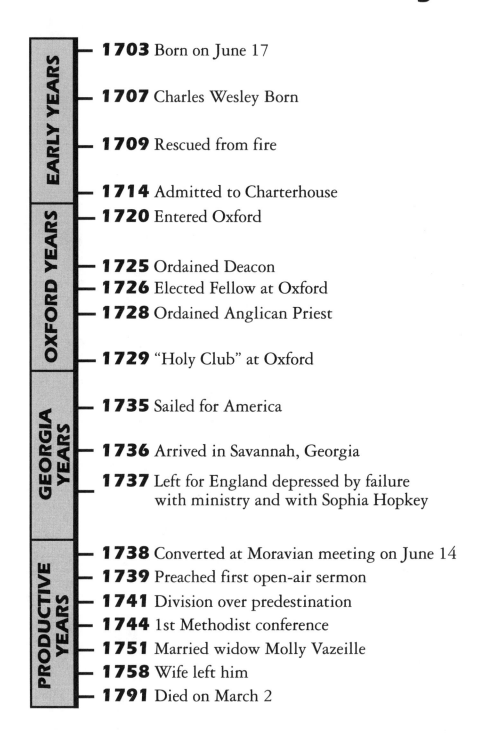

EARLY YEARS

1703 Born on June 17

1707 Charles Wesley Born

1709 Rescued from fire

1714 Admitted to Charterhouse

OXFORD YEARS

1720 Entered Oxford

1725 Ordained Deacon
1726 Elected Fellow at Oxford
1728 Ordained Anglican Priest

1729 "Holy Club" at Oxford

GEORGIA YEARS

1735 Sailed for America

1736 Arrived in Savannah, Georgia

1737 Left for England depressed by failure with ministry and with Sophia Hopkey

PRODUCTIVE YEARS

1738 Converted at Moravian meeting on June 14
1739 Preached first open-air sermon
1741 Division over predestination
1744 1st Methodist conference
1751 Married widow Molly Vazeille
1758 Wife left him
1791 Died on March 2

One of the foremost leaders of the eighteenth century English revival was John Benjamin Wesley. He was born into the home of an Anglican cleric and was educated at Christ Church College, Oxford. In Oxford he became involved with a Pietist group called the Holy Club. In the 1730s he sailed to the British colony in Georgia where he served as a missionary. Returning in 1738 under stressful conditions, Wesley experienced a religious renewal in a Moravian meeting at Aldersgate Street. He devoted the remainder of his long life seeking to bring renewal to the churches of England.

Chart 47

THE PERIOD OF THE BRITISH SETTLEMENT IN NORTH AMERICA: THE COLONIAL PERIOD OF AMERICAN RELIGIOUS HISTORY (1600 to 1800)

Backgrounds of American Religious History

Winthrop Hudson's Interpretation of American Religious History

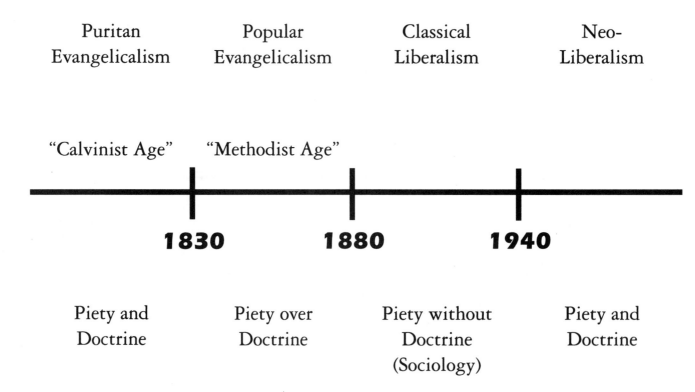

Puritan Evangelicalism

Popular Evangelicalism

Classical Liberalism

Neo-Liberalism

"Calvinist Age"   "Methodist Age"

1830   **1880**   **1940**

Piety and Doctrine

Piety over Doctrine

Piety without Doctrine (Sociology)

Piety and Doctrine

Prominent Baptist historian Winthrop Hudson divided American religious history into four segments. In this view, changes in religious life occurred in the 1830s with the decline of Puritanism and the increasing popularity of democratic influences on culture. This changed with the coming of Protestant Liberalism in the 1880s, which he viewed negatively. A more balanced view of religion prevailed in the 1940s with the restructuring of the American liberal movement by Neoliberalism. In his view this meant that religious life and teaching were once again harmoniously coordinated.

Chart 48

H. Richard Niebuhr's Interpretation of American Religious History

	Kingdom of Divine Sovereignty	Kingdom of Christ	Kingdom on Earth

1830   1880

	Kingdom of Divine Sovereignty	Kingdom of Christ	Kingdom on Earth
MAJOR MOTIF	Theocracy	Revivalism	Social Gospel
TRUTH BASE	Bible	Reason	Existentialism
MAJOR CHARACTERISTICS	Sovereignty Grace Humanitarianism	Grace Sovereignty Humanitarianism	Grace Humanitarianism Sovereignty

Richard Niehbur, a neoliberal scholar, interpreted American Religious history through the grid of the emergence of the Kingdom of God in human history, a popular theme in the 1930s. American history has passed through three stages, each a step in the right direction from the previous one. American religion has become more gracious and kindly disposed via revivalism, away from the harsher themes of Puritan Calvinism.

Chart 49

Sidney Ahlstrom's Interpretation of American Religious History

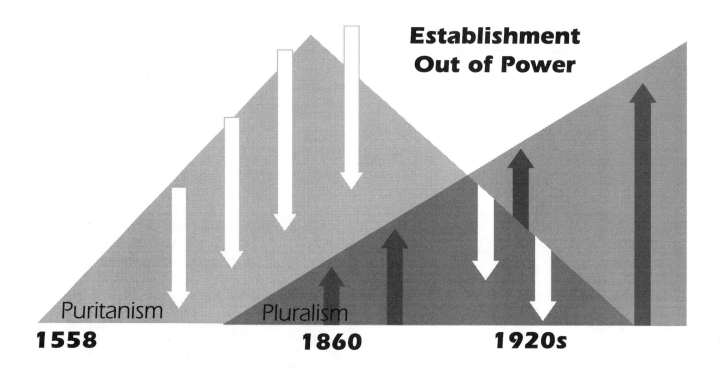

Establishment Out of Power

Puritanism

Pluralism

1558

1860

1920s

BEGINNING OF PURITAN EPOCH

BEGINNING OF AMERICAN COLONIZATION

END OF PURITAN EPOCH

The grandest interpretation of American religion has been that of Sidney Ahlstrom. He saw two antithetical forces vying for dominance in American religion: Christianity (which he calls Puritanism) and Pluralism or secularism. Puritanism was dominant in American religious life until the twentieth century. By 1900 the influence of secularism equaled that of Christianity. By 1920 pluralism was the dominant influence. In the turmoil of the 1960s, Christianity no longer influenced the direction of American culture.

Chart 50

Bruce Shelley's Interpretation of American Religious History

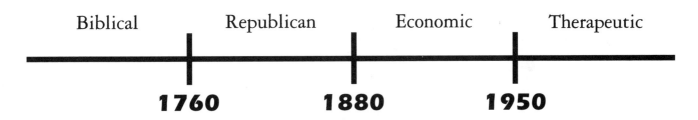

Biblical | Republican | Economic | Therapeutic

1760 | 1880 | 1950

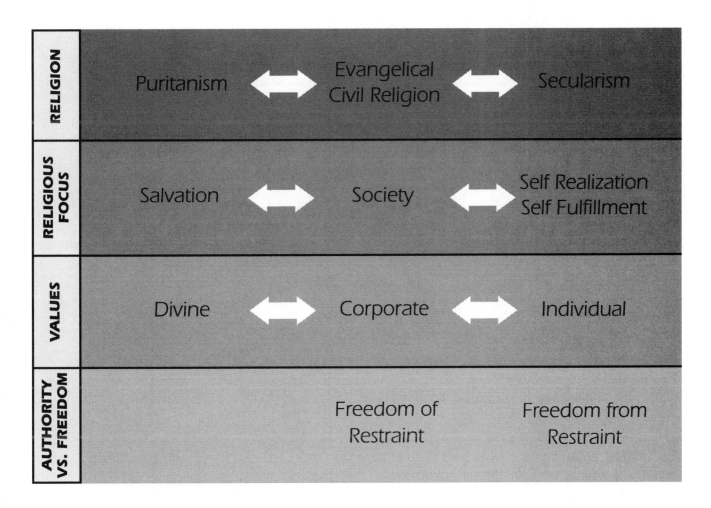

RELIGION	Puritanism ⟷	Evangelical Civil Religion ⟷	Secularism
RELIGIOUS FOCUS	Salvation ⟷	Society ⟷	Self Realization Self Fulfillment
VALUES	Divine ⟷	Corporate ⟷	Individual
AUTHORITY VS. FREEDOM		Freedom of Restraint	Freedom from Restraint

A recent religious historian, Bruce Shelley, divided the story of American religion into four parts. He viewed the era of British colonialism as deeply Christian in nature, but subsequent eras as increasingly less so, until secularity became dominant in the 1950s. Corporate nationalism, like the religious conservatism of the colonial era that undergirded it, has vanished. Secularism, the absence of absolute moral values, and individualism dominate current American cultural values.

Chart 51

John Hannah's Interpretation of American Religious History

THEME: The Kingdom of Enlightened Man

	Age of Divine Sovereignty	Age of Biblicistic Rationalism	Age of Rationalism, Science	Age of Privatism, Self
Historical Structure	COLONIAL PERIOD	NATIONAL PERIOD	MODERN PERIOD	POSTMODERN PERIOD
Truth Base	Theocentrism	Biblicistic Rationalism	Rationalism	Individualism
Historical Motif	Migration	National Birth	Maturation	Uncertainty, anxiety, randomness

Timeline markers: 1760, 1880, 1960

Chart 52

The author interprets American religious history through the lenses of both Sidney Ahlstrom and Bruce Shelley. The story of Christianity is one of decline from a belief in the absolute sovereignty of God over all of life to the rampant secularism that prevails in current American culture. This tremendous change has been brought about by the decline of a God-centered faith.

Sources of the American Religious Experience

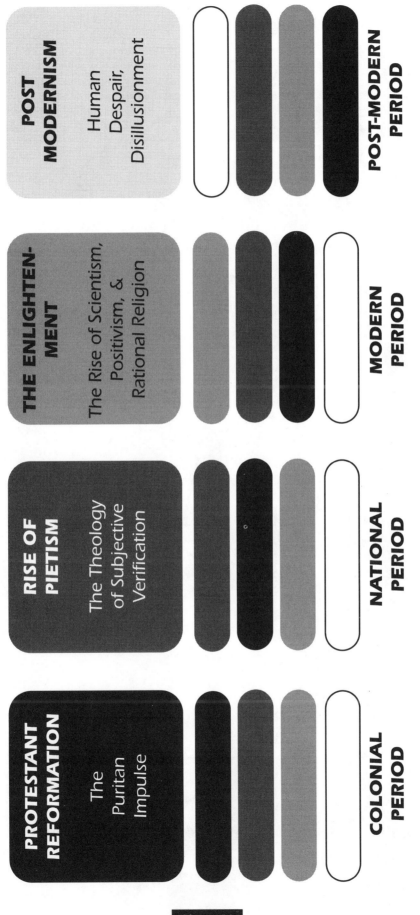

PROTESTANT REFORMATION

The Puritan Impulse

COLONIAL PERIOD

RISE OF PIETISM

The Theology of Subjective Verification

NATIONAL PERIOD

THE ENLIGHTEN-MENT

The Rise of Scientism, Positivism, & Rational Religion

MODERN PERIOD

POST MODERNISM

Human Despair, Disillusionment

POST-MODERN PERIOD

American Christianity has been shaped by four impulses. The Protestant Reformation dominated the colonial era, evangelical pietism and revivalism the period between the Revolution and the Civil War, the Enlightenment as represented by Protestant liberalism from the 1900s to the 1950s, and secularism since. This chart shows the most important influence and the least felt influence in each era of American religious history.

Chart 53

Old World Denominational Origins in British America

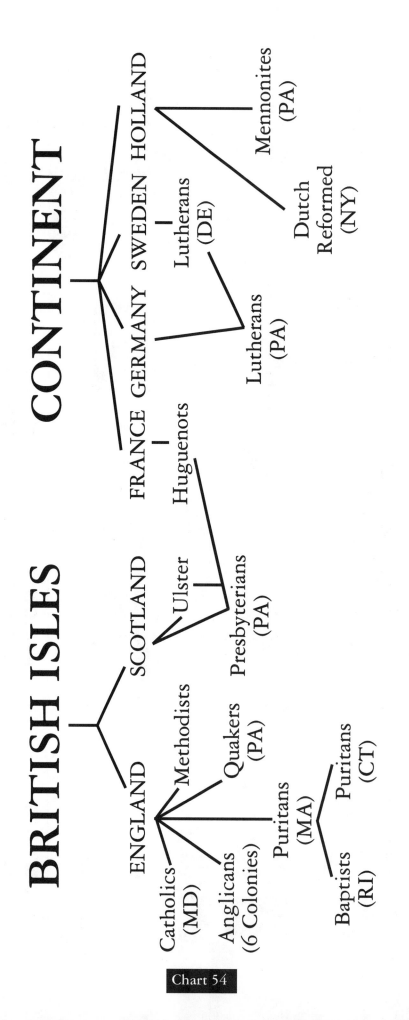

BRITISH ISLES

ENGLAND
- Catholics (MD)
- Methodists
- Anglicans (6 Colonies)
- Quakers (PA)
- Puritans (MA)
  - Baptists (RI)
  - Puritans (CT)

SCOTLAND
- Ulster
  - Presbyterians (PA)

CONTINENT

FRANCE
- Huguenots

GERMANY

SWEDEN

HOLLAND
- Lutherans (DE)
- Lutherans (PA)
- Dutch Reformed (NY)
- Mennonites (PA)

Chart 54

The origins of the various religious faiths that settled in the British colonies were of English and Northern European heritage. Congregationalists, Presbyterians, Anglicans, Quakers, and the later Methodists came from the British Isles. Baptists had both continental and British roots. Mennonites, Moravians, and Huguenots, among others, were of European origin.

Congregationalists

Congregationalism in America

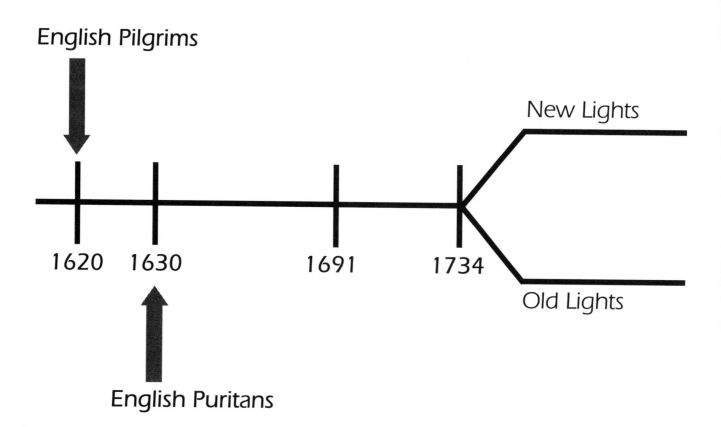

The Congregationalists were composed of two distinct groups. Puritan Pilgrims arrived in the early 1620s and settled at Plymouth. These people had first fled from England to Holland. The larger and vastly more influential group were Puritans who left England after 1629 and came directly to New England, settling in Charleston, Boston, and elsewhere. The Great Awakening (1726–60) brought schism: the "Old Lights," led by Charles Chauncy, opposed the revivals, the "New Lights," under Jonathan Edwards.

Chart 55

Denominationalism in New England

England   America

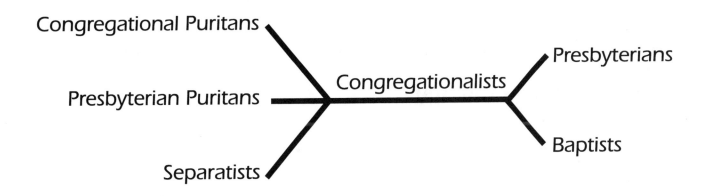

The Puritans, the dissenters from the Church of England who "swarmed" into New England, were not uniform in their theological preferences. When Congregationalists, Presbyterians, and Separatists arrived, they coalesced to conform to Congregationalism. Two areas make this evident: franchise and church polity. In the area of franchise, Thomas Hooker and Roger Williams believed that the right to vote should be broader than was permitted in Boston and its environs. In the area of church polity, some Puritans would have liked a Presbyterian government, others a Congregational form, and still others a blending of the two. Congregationalism prevailed for a time in the New England churches. Over the next several generations those with Presbyterian and Baptist leanings emerged to their original preferences.

Chart 56

John Cotton and the Puritan Errand in History

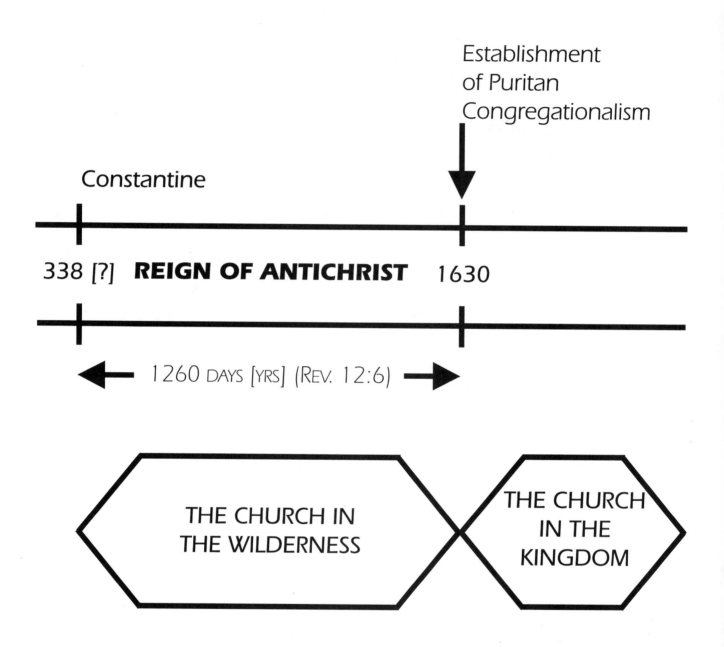

Establishment
of Puritan
Congregationalism

Constantine

338 [?] **REIGN OF ANTICHRIST** 1630

← 1260 DAYS [YRS] (REV. 12:6) →

THE CHURCH IN
THE WILDERNESS

THE CHURCH
IN THE
KINGDOM

John Cotton, the foremost early clergyman in the colony, was a student of the book of Revelation. From his study of the book, he concluded that the kingdom of God had arrived with the settling of the Puritans in the New World. The time of Constantine to 1630 was the period of the church in the wilderness. The great promised day had dawned. This perspective gave the Puritans a sense of hope.

Chart 57

The Antinomian Controversy

ARMINIANS	CALVINISTS	ANTINOMIANS
Life of Progressive Growth in the Spirit	Immediacy of Experience	Immediacy of Experience
	Life of Progressive Growth in the Spirit	

The essence of Anne Hutchinson's complaint was her accusation that the clergy were teaching a salvation by works because they insisted that works were necessary for assurance of salvation. She argued that assurance of salvation is rooted solely in the inner witness of the Spirit, while the clergy said that assurance is based on the witness of the Bible and the work of the Spirit in transforming lives. She was called an "antinominian" because of her insistence that keeping the law was not a ground of assurance.

Chart 58

"The Mania of 1692": The Salem Witch Trials

Human, Natural ⟶ Cause	Human, ⟵ Supernatural Cause	Supernatural Cause
Psychological Stress, Societal Conflict, Ergot Poisoning, Ministerial Fright	Witchcraft (*Humans in League with the Devil Afflicting Humans*) Therefore: A Witch Hunt	Demonic Possession

One of the most infamous episodes in Puritan history was the Salem Witch Trials of the 1690s. The view of the day was that the affliction of Samuel Parris's daughter and several others was caused by colonists who were in league with the devil. Had this been the case, a witch hunt would have been appropriate. Some recent historians have tried to find a sociological root for it. Others have suggested that the problem stemmed from demonic influence exerted through the girls and that the accused were actually the innocent.

Chart 59

The Puritans:
The Interconnectedness
of Church and State

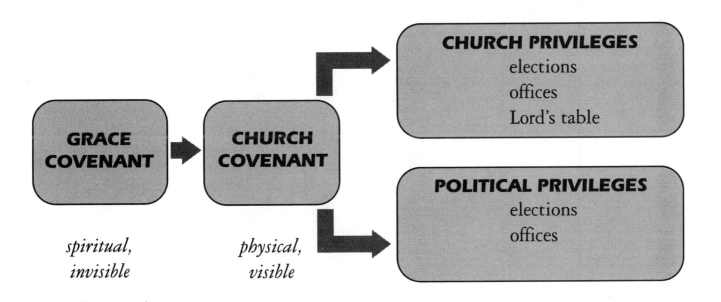

GRACE
COVENANT

*spiritual,
invisible*

CHURCH
COVENANT

*physical,
visible*

CHURCH PRIVILEGES
elections
offices
Lord's table

POLITICAL PRIVILEGES
elections
offices

In the Puritan worldview, church and state were intertwined. In fact, political privilege in Massachusetts was linked to being a church member. The church covenant was an outward sign that one had embraced the invisible covenant of grace. Without the external symbol of divine relationship, one had neither church-membership privileges nor civil privileges. However, there were strictly enforced religious codes for everyone in the colony.

Chart 60

The Puritan Dream

The Hope of the Puritan Dream	The Child's Case & Cambridge Platform	Halfway Covenant	Stoddard-eanism	Salem Witch Trials	Massachusetts Proposals	The End of the Hope of the Puritan Dream
	1646–48	1662	1677	1692	1705	

Decline of Puritan Utopianism

Chart 61

The Puritans had the dream of establishing "a city set upon a hill." The dream entailed a Bible Commonwealth and was rooted in the great promise that God unconditionally made with Abraham to bless him and his posterity. The dream of an elect nation became increasingly difficult to maintain as subsequent generations were not as enthusiastic to enter into full church membership. To maintain the hope of the "city," Puritan leadership found it necessary to redefine the ideal citizen through the Halfway Covenant and the innovations of Solomon Stoddard.

Education in Puritan New England

Private Education

Reading
Writing

Grammar School Latin

"teaching of grammar, rhetoric, and arithmetic,
and the tongues of Latin, Greek, and Hebrew,
also to read English and to write." (Morison, p. 98)

College

(Language of instruction: Latin)

Arts: Grammar, Logic, Rhetoric, Arithmetic,
Geometry, and Astronomy.

Philosophies: Metaphysics, Ethics,
and Natural Science.

Also: Greek, Hebrew and Ancient History

The Puritans of New England were profoundly interested in education. They mandated that children must learn to read and write the native tongue, and they established free public education with the "Old Deluder Act" of 1643. Further, they established grammar schools for the study of Latin, which was a prerequisite for entrance into the emerging colleges, where Latin was the language of instruction. The literacy rate was extremely high among the Puritans.

Chart 62

Sources of American Puritan Theology

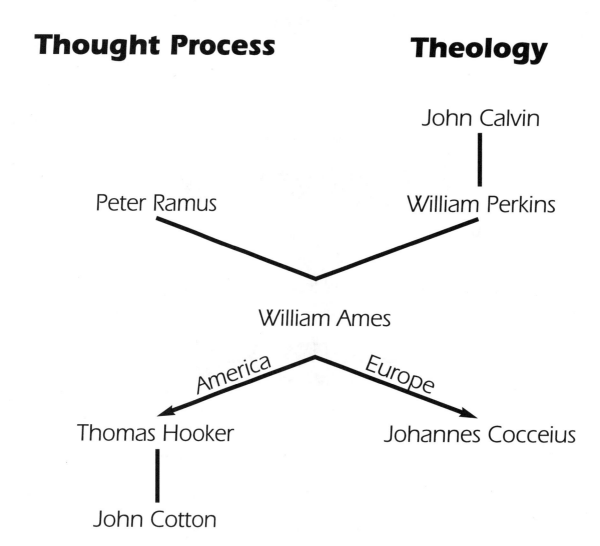

Thought Process

Theology

John Calvin

Peter Ramus

William Perkins

William Ames

America

Europe

Thomas Hooker

Johannes Cocceius

John Cotton

While the Puritan world was rooted in the *Institutes of Christian Religion* by John Calvin, the more immediate influences on them were William Perkins (1558–1602), the Oxford writer of *The Golden Chain;* Johannes Cocceius (or Koch) (1479–1552), the Dutch systematizer of covenantal theology; and William Ames (1576–1633). It was the latter's *Medulla of Sacred Theology* that was a textbook at Harvard College.

Chart 63

Indian Missions and the American Puritan

WORKERS	TRIBE	AREA
1 Rev. Fitch	Pequots	N.E. Connecticut
2 Rev. Pierson	Mohegans	S.E. Connecticut
3 Roger Williams	Narragansetts	Rhode Island
4 Mayhews	Pawkunnawkutts	Martha's Vineyard
5 John Eliot	Massachusetts	Mass. Bay
6 Rich Bourne	Pawtucketts	N.E. Mass.
7 Rich Bourne	Algonquins	Vermont
8 John Sargeant	Houstatonnocs	W. Mass.

The Puritans viewed the Indians with ambivalence. They were the object of fear and rage at times, as well as easy prey for injustice. However, some Puritans looked upon them with a missionary passion. Before King Philip's War of the 1670s, the story of missionary work is inspiring. The cleric John Eliot was eminently successful in converting them. After that devastating war, which turned many to treat the Indian as an object of revenge, and in the context of the Great Awakening of the 1700s, the labors of David Brainerd inspired world missions in the nineteenth century.

Chart 64

Indian Missions: The Mayhew Family and Martha's Vineyard

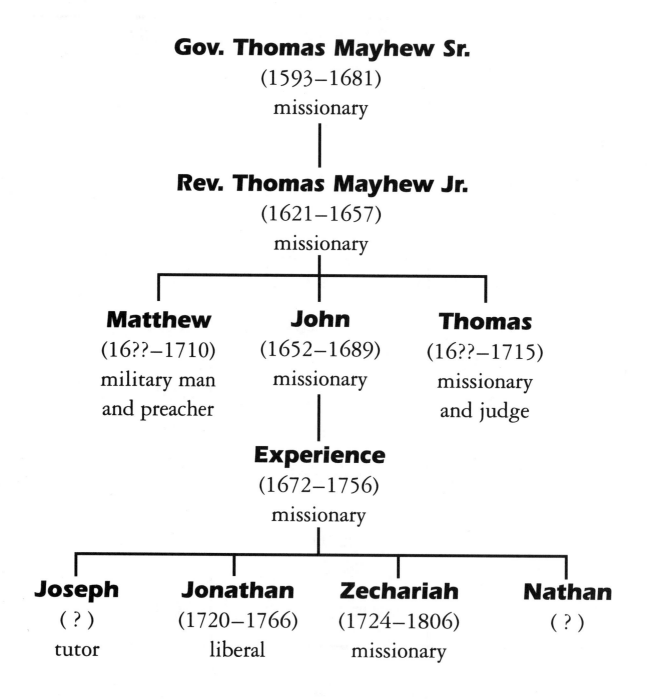

Gov. Thomas Mayhew Sr.
(1593–1681)
missionary

Rev. Thomas Mayhew Jr.
(1621–1657)
missionary

Matthew
(16??–1710)
military man
and preacher

John
(1652–1689)
missionary

Thomas
(16??–1715)
missionary
and judge

Experience
(1672–1756)
missionary

Joseph
(?)
tutor

Jonathan
(1720–1766)
liberal

Zechariah
(1724–1806)
missionary

Nathan
(?)

The story of one remarkable family is particularly interesting, the Mayhew Family of Martha's Vineyard. Starting with Thomas Mayhew, son of the island's governor, generations of Mayhews labored for the souls of American Indians. Perhaps a harbinger of changing times was Jonathan Mayhew, who left the religious Puritanism of his forebears for Unitarianism and political activism.

Chart 65

Baptists

Origins of Baptists in America

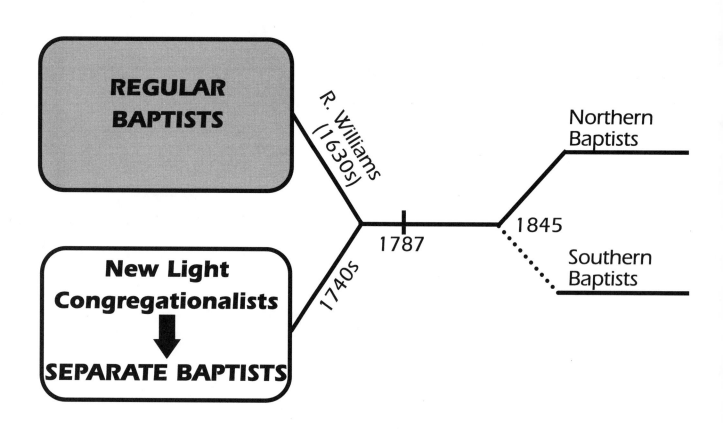

The Baptists have two sources in British America. The earliest Baptists who came to Rhode Island from England, and in larger numbers to the Middle colonies from Europe, were of Particular or Calvinistic orientation. They are often designated as Regular Baptists to indicate that they came to the colonies with Baptist doctrine. A second source is to be found among the Congregationalists in the Great Awakening of the 1740s. Because they separated from Congregationalism they were known as Separate Baptists. These two groups gradually merged. The Southern Baptists later withdrew over the issue of slavery.

Chart 66

The Religious Affiliations of Roger Williams

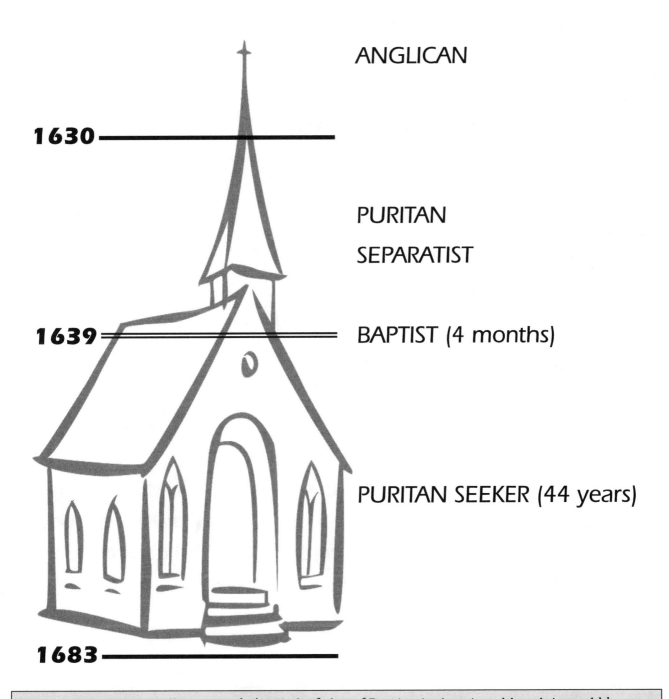

ANGLICAN

1630 ———————

PURITAN

SEPARATIST

1639 ═══════ BAPTIST (4 months)

PURITAN SEEKER (44 years)

1683 ———————

Many consider Roger Williams (c. 1604–83) the father of Baptists in America, although it would be more accurate to say that he founded the first colony that welcomed Baptists in the New World. Williams came into Massachusetts in 1630, moved on to Salem, and eventually settled in Plymouth, where he learned the Indian language and wrote a primer. He resettled in Boston for a time, but his political views caused trouble. Banished from the colony he settled Providence in 1636, and gained the charter for Rhode Island in 1643. He created a colony with broad religious freedoms.

Chart 67

The Millennialism of Roger Williams

Beginning of Christ's Reign

Corruption of Christ's Reign

Renewal of Christ's Reign

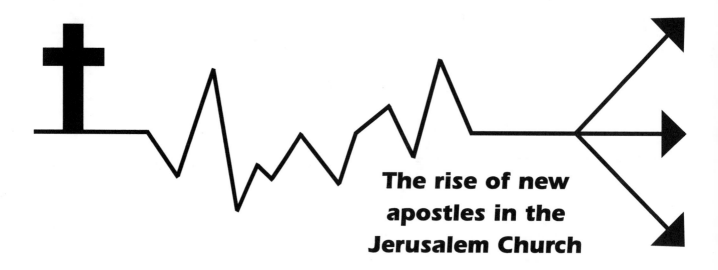

The rise of new apostles in the Jerusalem Church

1. Churches and ordinances corrupt
2. Governments evil
3. Godly commonwealth impossible
4. Gospel preaching (missions) irrelevant and unnecessary

Christ reigning in truly reformed churches

Williams' views were often contrary to those of his Puritan neighbors. He believed that the church at the time of Constantine in the fourth century was corrupted by entanglement with the state and remained that way. Therefore, any attempt to establish a godly society was doomed to failure, and all churches and sacraments were corrupt. Gospel preaching was fruitless until prophets came from Jerusalem to establish a pure church once again. To the dismay of the Puritans in Massachusetts, Williams was sure that Boston was not the kingdom of God.

Chart 68

Turning Points in the History of Baptists in America

The First Great Awakening		The American Revolution		The Second Great Awakening
	⬅➡		⬅➡	
deliverance from numerical obscurity		deliverance from intolerance		deliverance unto religious prominence

The history of the Baptists in early America can be described in relation to three significant events: two religious awakenings and the American Revolution. Between the two awakenings that brought significant numerical growth, the revolution and the establishment of a new government delivered them from religious restrictions and intolerance.

Chart 69

Presbyterians

The Origins of Presbyterianism in North America

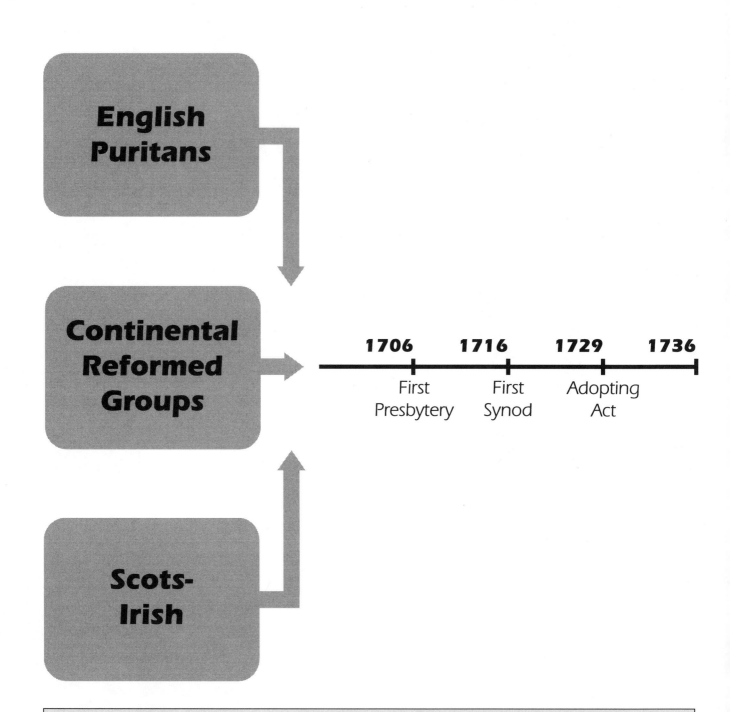

English Puritans

Continental Reformed Groups

Scots-Irish

1706 — First Presbytery

1716 — First Synod

1729 — Adopting Act

1736

Many Presbyterians came from England in the "swarming of the Puritans" to New England. However, because of the dominance of Congregationalism, those of Presbyterian sympathy were faced with the choice between conformity in silence or moving to more hospitable places. Some Presbyterians came from continental roots such as the Huguenots or Germans from the Palatinate. The majority of Presbyterians were Scots-Irish, who came from Scotland via Ireland.

Chart 70

The Ecclesiastical Structure of Presbyterianism

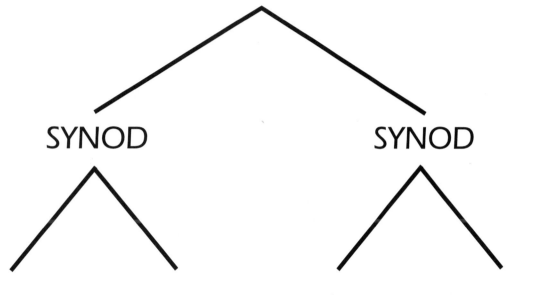

NATIONAL ASSEMBLY

SYNOD   SYNOD

PRESBYTERY   PRESBYTERY   PRESBYTERY   PRESBYTERY

SESSION   SESSION

Presbyterianism is a republican, representative form of church government. Above the individual sessions of each church is an administrative body called the presbytery, which consists of pastors and teaching elders from the churches in a region; it handles questions of church concerns and ordains clergy for the churches. Several presbyteries in a large region compose a synod. Representatives from the synods make up the General or National Assembly.

Chart 71

Methodists

The Birth of American Methodism

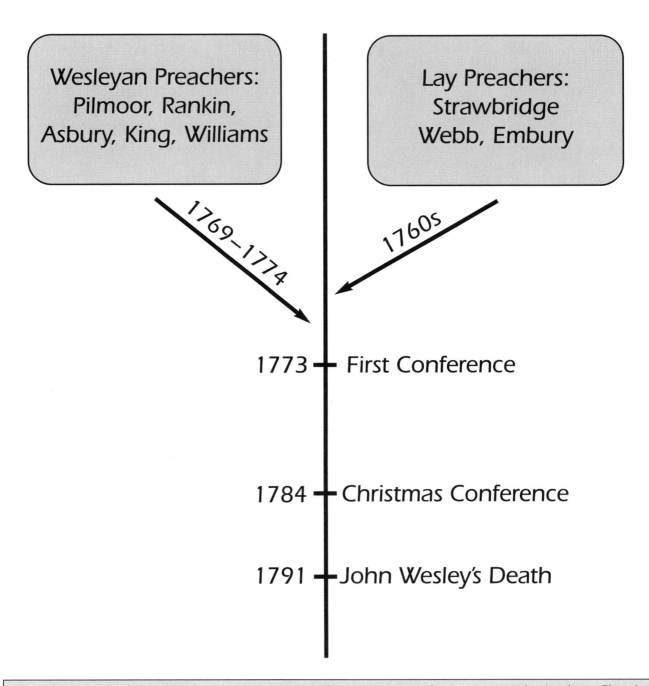

Wesleyan Preachers:
Pilmoor, Rankin,
Asbury, King, Williams

Lay Preachers:
Strawbridge
Webb, Embury

1769–1774

1760s

1773 — First Conference

1784 — Christmas Conference

1791 — John Wesley's Death

Methodism was established in the British American colonies as a renewal movement in the Anglican Church. Methodists were initially brought into the church by lay preachers. These lay preachers were quite successful, and Wesley reasoned that trained leadership had the potential of even greater success. Between 1769 and 1774 Wesley appointed twelve seasoned British circuit riders.

With the success of Wesley's circuit preachers, Methodism was born at the Baltimore Conference in 1773. Methodism in America officially severed its ties with the Anglican Church in 1784, at which time the Methodist Episcopal Church was born.

Chart 72

Francis Asbury's Circuit

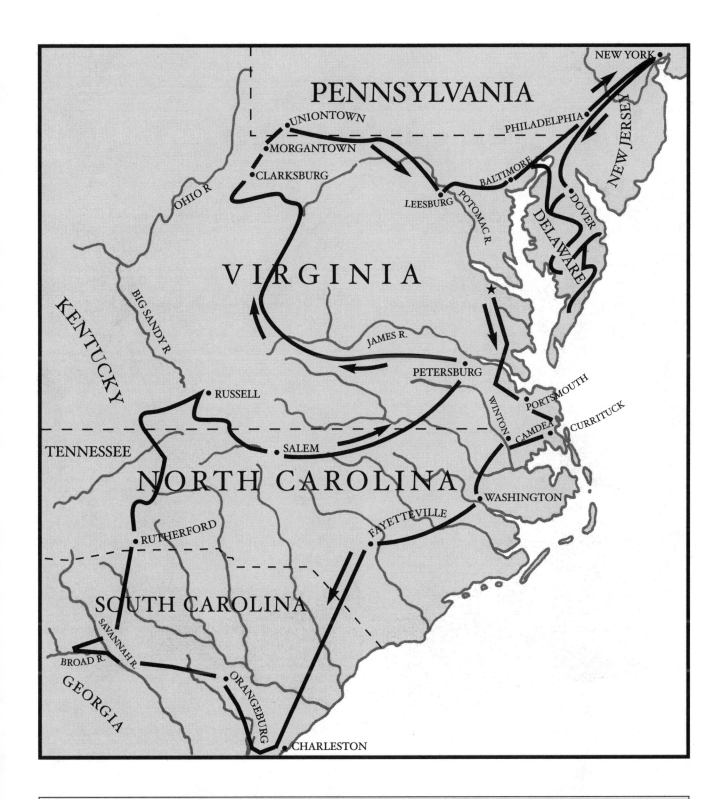

Francis Asbury was a tireless worker for the establishment of Methodism in the new American nation. His circuit extended from New York to Georgia along the coast and into the backcountry. It is said that he visited every Methodist society in America twice yearly. He truly is the "Father of American Methodism".

Chart 73

The Ecclesiastical Structure of Methodism

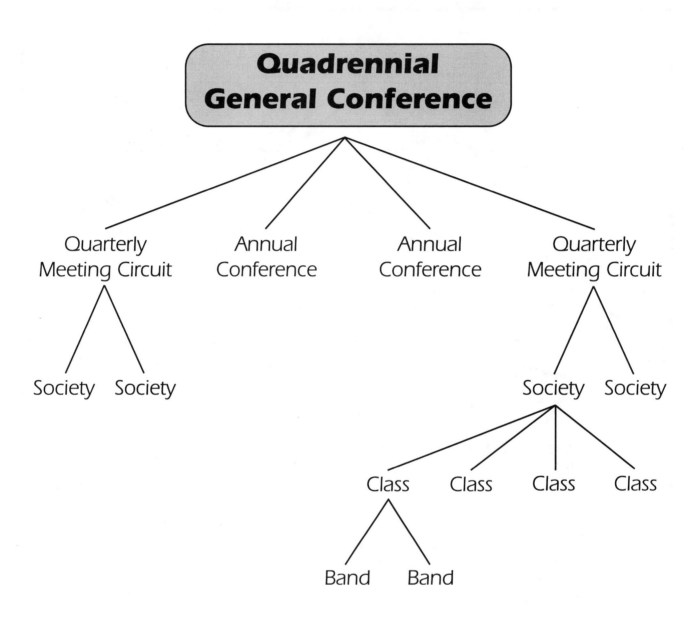

Following the British pattern, American Methodism was highly structured. The earliest Methodists called their gatherings *societies*. Each society was subdivided into classes for small-group Bible study, and these were further subdivided for prayer. There were no local pastors. Instead, regions were divided into circuits and itinerant preachers cared for the scattered societies. The societies within a circuit would gather quarterly in a camp meeting. Several circuits made up a conference, which met yearly to handle business. Every four years representatives from all the conferences met in a general or national conference.

Chart 74

Quakers

The Ecclesiastical Structure of the Quakers

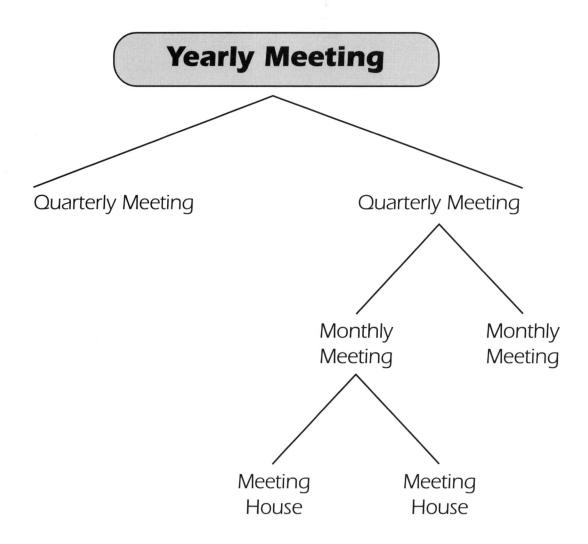

Yearly Meeting

Quarterly Meeting

Quarterly Meeting

Monthly Meeting

Monthly Meeting

Meeting House

Meeting House

The Quakers were not hospitably received, except in the Middle Colonies and Charleston. Their views of church worship (the role of women, inner light, rejection of the need for pastors, rejection of the sacraments) as well as political pacifism made them a minority. Quakers, however, did flourish throughout the colonies and established an intricate ecclesiastical structure.

Chart 75

Lutherans

The Origins of Lutheranism in America

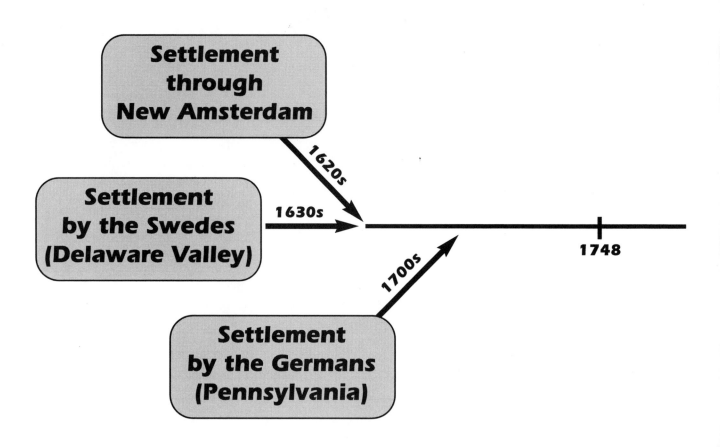

The Lutheran presence in the American colonies was that of a Protestant minority, at least until the nineteenth century. Lutherans did come into the colony in three ways: through New York, then owned by the Dutch (who themselves were Calvinists); through the Swedes that settled in southern New Jersey; and through the Germans that came into Pennsylvania. The latter was the largest group. Henry Muhlenberg organized the Lutheran churches throughout Pennsylvania and emerged as a church leader in 1748.

Chart 76

The Great Awakening

The History of Awakenings in America

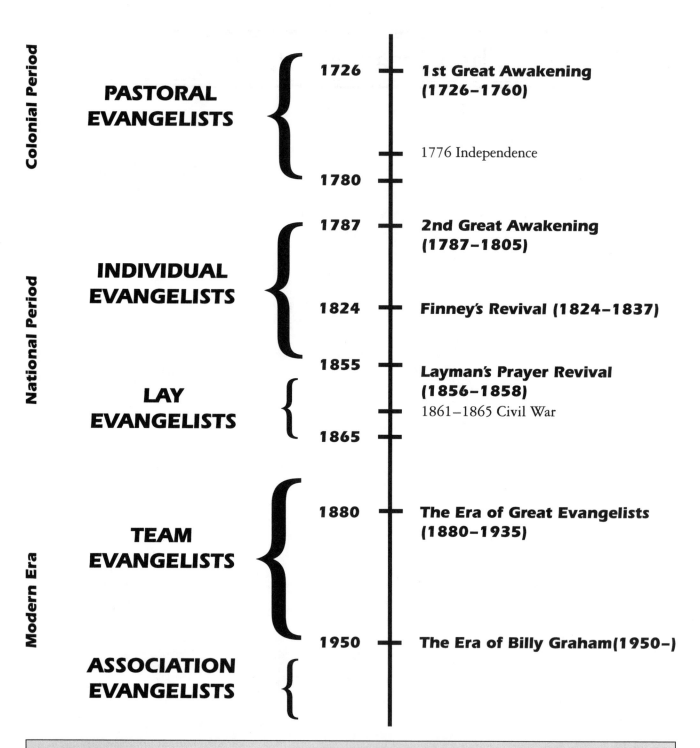

Colonial Period

PASTORAL EVANGELISTS

1726 — **1st Great Awakening (1726–1760)**

1776 Independence

1780

National Period

INDIVIDUAL EVANGELISTS

1787 — **2nd Great Awakening (1787–1805)**

1824 — **Finney's Revival (1824–1837)**

1855 — **Layman's Prayer Revival (1856–1858)**

LAY EVANGELISTS

1861–1865 Civil War

1865

Modern Era

TEAM EVANGELISTS

1880 — **The Era of Great Evangelists (1880–1935)**

1950 — **The Era of Billy Graham (1950–)**

ASSOCIATION EVANGELISTS

Scholars have identified six periods of intense religious activity in American history. One occurred in the Colonial Era, three in the National Era, and two in the Modern Era. The periods of revival or awakening that appear to have had the greatest impact were the first two awakenings and the Layman's Prayer Revival of 1858. The history of evangelism in America bears witness to changes that parallel these events.

Chart 77

The History of Mass Evangelism in America

REVIVALISTIC	EVANGELISTIC

2nd Awakening (1787–1805)
AND
Finney (1824–1837)

MEANS

Invisible

Visible
Invisible

RESULTS

Revival

Individual
Conversions

Charles Finney is a watershed in the history of evangelism in America. Not only did he bring various techniques to the work of gathering souls, his theology was quite novel, if not Pelagian. After Finney it seems that evangelists became enamored with response more than with the proclamation of the gospel message itself.

Chart 78

The First Great Awakening

Middle Colonies
Frelinghausen G. Tennent

New England
Frontier Phase   Whitefieldian Phase

Southern Colonies
Presbyterians

Baptists

Anglican-Methodist

| 1710 | 1720 | 1730 | 1740 | 1750 | 1760 | 1770 | 1780 | 1790 |

Jonathan Edwards
Northampton Stockbridge   Princeton

George Whitefield
America →

The First Great Awakening (1720s–1760s) may be summarized as having three phases and two dominant figures. It began in the Middle Colonies through the preaching of Theodore Frelinghausen and spread among the Presbyterians. In New England, it began in 1734–35 in Jonathan Edwards' church and spread down the Connecticur River Valley. In 1740–42 a more widely fruitful awakening was the result of the itinerant preaching of George Whitefield. In the southern colonies of the 1750s the revival was widespread among the Presbyterians, Baptists, and Anglicans that gradually became Methodists.

Chart 79

The First Great Awakening and the Presbyterian Church

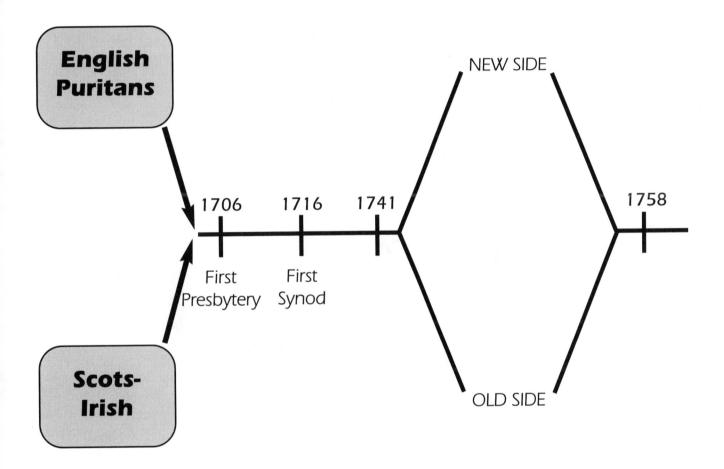

The Great Awakening among the Presbyterians brought the church close to a schism. Some viewed the awakening as positive; others feared the negative effects of emotional extremism and itinerancy. In 1741 the Presbyterians polarized into two parties, with many seeking a middle road between them. Those who favored the awakening were the New Siders, who identified with the emerging College of New Jersey (Princeton). The Old Siders were concentrated in Philadelphia and favored moderation. When the awakening ceased, the tensions faded and the two parties put aside their differences.

Chart 80

Jonathan Edwards' View of the Soul

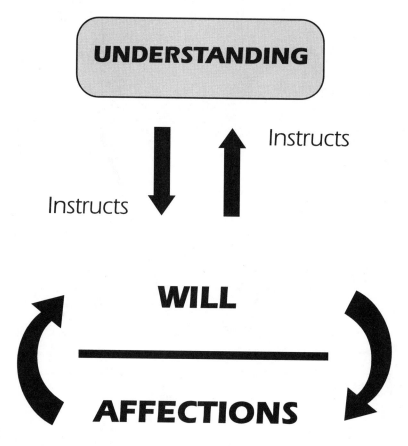

Jonathan Edwards believed that the immaterial part of man was twofold: Mind or understanding and will or inclinations. The deepest part of the soul was the affections; it is in the affections that regeneration happens. Information impressed upon the mind instructs the will based on what it likes or dislikes (the affections) which results in choices. To Edwards, mankind is both a rational and an affectional being. Preaching, to be effective, must reach not only the cognitive part of man, but the affections as well. Unlike his Puritan forebears, who viewed the faculties of the soul as arranged in a linear causative order, Edwards saw them as deeply interrelated.

Chart 81

Chauncy vs. Edwards: The Nature of Salvation

	EDWARDS	CHAUNCY
FOCUS:	The senses (affective apprehension, the heart)	The mind
OBTAINMENT:	Immediate	Mediate (means of grace)
CAUSATIVE MIRACLE:	Mercy of God	God-given rational ability
DOCTRINE OF ASSURANCE:	Based on experience (conversion sustains its own authenticity)	Based on attendance to means
DOCTRINE OF ITINERACY:	Approved	Abhorred

Edwards defended the Great Awakening as a genuine work of the Lord against people to his right (the enthusiasts) and to his left (the rationalists). He believed that religion with light but lack of emotion was just as unbiblical as emotion without light or a solid biblical basis. To define both his defense of the awakening and the unease he felt with certain features of it, he wrote *A Treatise on Religious Affections* (1746). Edwards opposed Charles Chauncy, whose views were quite different from those held by Edwards.

Chart 82

The First Great Awakening and New England Congregationalism

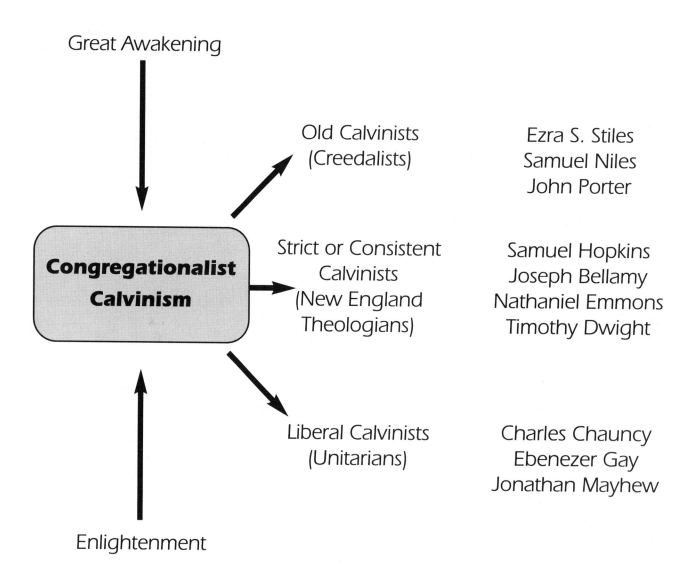

Great Awakening

Congregationalist Calvinism

Old Calvinists
(Creedalists)

Ezra S. Stiles
Samuel Niles
John Porter

Strict or Consistent
Calvinists
(New England
Theologians)

Samuel Hopkins
Joseph Bellamy
Nathaniel Emmons
Timothy Dwight

Liberal Calvinists
(Unitarians)

Charles Chauncy
Ebenezer Gay
Jonathan Mayhew

Enlightenment

The Great Awakening on the one hand and Enlightenment rationalism on the other split Congregationalism. Liberal Calvinists adopted the Enlightenment understanding of truth and reasonability, abandoning the historic Christian faith for Unitarianism. Others—called Old Calvinists—made no adjustments to the Enlightenment and went about preaching traditional Calvinist doctrine. Still others sought areas on adjustment to the Enlightenment that would allow the faith to be defended against rationalist attacks yet remain intact and relevant to the new American nation. These were called New Divinity or New England theologians.

Chart 83

Religion and the
American Revolution

The Revolutions in America and France Compared

	American 1776	**French** 1789
FOUNDATION	Locke (*Treatises on Government*, 1689)	Voltaire Rousseau Diderot
NATURE	Mild	Radical
CAUSE	Enchantment with rationalism	Disillusion with rationalism

Though there are connections between the American Revolution and the later French Revolution, there were also differences. From a philosophical viewpoint, American leaders were influenced by John Locke's notions of political entitlement and Scottish Common Sense moral philosophy, not radical ideologies. Americans were enchanted with the virtues of Enlightenment rationalism while the French were disillusioned with it. Optimism prevailed in America, pessimism in France.

Chart 84

The Enlightenment, Religion, and the Birth of the Nation

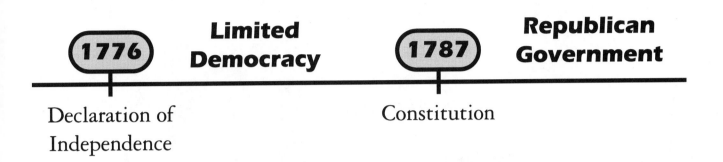

Limited Democracy   **Republican Government**

(1776)   (1787)

Declaration of Independence   Constitution

ENLIGHTENED RATIONALISM

The great documents of the new nation, the Declaration of Independence and the Constitution, reflect a deep religious commitment—but not necessarily a truly Christian one. The founders of the new nation, at the national level, were Unitarians, Deists, and Christians. They created documents that affirm the existence of God and divine rights, but religion was prized as a moral glue for the new American culture. The political theory expressed in the founding documents demonstrates an entitlement of rights more reflective of Enlightenment rationalism than of Christianity with its more sober view of human ability.

Chart 85

Christianity and the Enlightenment: Agreement on Goals for Different Reasons

To Protect the Elect
(Man Evil)

Separation of Church and State

1775

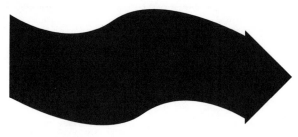

To Permit Man to be Autonomous
(Man Good)

It is something of a puzzlement that in the construction of the new nation Christians and rationalists could find significant agreement of purpose in the context of significant religious differences. Both sought separation from England and embraced the same documents of state—but for vastly different reasons. Christians favored separation from England to protect themselves from evil; the rationalists sought to found a nation characterized by freedom, believing that autonomy would promote the essential goodness of man and prove that man possessed the ability to govern wisely without the imposition of external authority.

Chart 86

Thomas Jefferson and Benjamin Franklin

Thomas Jefferson, Religion, and the Nation

8 January 1825

Letter, Thomas Jefferson to Benjamin Waterhouse

"Had the doctrines of Jesus been preached always as pure as they came from his lips, the whole civilized world would now have been Christian. I rejoice that in this blessed country of free inquiry and belief, which has surrendered its creed and conscience to neither kings nor priests, the genuine doctrine of one only God is reviving, and I trust that there is not a young man now living in the United States who will not die a Unitarian. The population of my neighborhood is too slender, and is too much divided into other sects to maintain any one preacher well. I must therefore be content to be a Unitarian by myself."

Thomas Jefferson and Christianity

27 September 1825

Letter, Thomas Jefferson to James Fishback

"Reading, reflection, and time have convinced me that the interests of society require the observation of those moral precepts only in which all religions agree [for all forbid us to murder, steal, plunder, or bear false witness], and that we should not intermeddle with the particular dogmas in which all religions differ, and which are totally unconnected with morality ... The varieties in the structure and action of the human mind as in those of the body are the work of our Creator, against which it cannot be religious duty to erect the standard of uniformity."

Thomas Jefferson, Morality, and Christianity

13 June 1814

Letter, Thomas Jefferson to Thomas Law

"Truth is certainly a branch of morality, and a very important one to society...Because nature hath implanted in breasts a love of others, a sense of duty to them, a moral instinct, in short, which prompts us irresistibly to feel and to succor their distresses ... nature has constituted utility to man the standard and test of virtue.

Benjamin Franklin on Christianity

"He who shall introduce into public affairs the principles of Christianity will change the face of the world."

Thomas Jefferson was, like John Adams, a Unitarian, who held that the essence of religion is moral virtue. Ideas such as the deity of Jesus are not the essence of true religion, but the morals displayed by Jesus, a Jewish peasant, are what is real.

Benjamin Franklin, a Deist, shared many of Jefferson's religious ideas. The essence of true religion is its ability to stimulate moral virtue, the glue of civil cohesion. It is not the doctrines of Christianity that make it Christian; it is its superior morals.

Chart 87

Unitarianism and Deism Compared

	UNITARIANISM	DEISM
PHILOSOPHICAL ORIENTATION:	Realism	Realism
EPISTEMOLOGY:	Empiricism, rationalism Reformation	Empiricism, rationalism
GOD:	Theistic: single, personal	Theistic: single, utterly transcendent
MEDIUM OF REVELATION:	Natural, supernatural	Natural
PERSON OF CHRIST:	Archetypical Man	Exemplary Man
NATURE OF SIN:	Personal depravity; Moral ability	Personal depravity; Moral ability
ATONEMENT:	Exemplary	(none)
SOURCES:	Reformation	Enlightenment

The line between Unitarianism and Deism was a thin one. They shared a common view of Jesus as a superior human being, but not more, and took an optimistic view of human potential. Both denied the need for a divine atonement for sin. The difference seems to have been that the Deist rejected the possibility of divine intervention into his world, preferring to think that natural law governed things (the watchmaker and watch image). Unitarians viewed God as a more personal than distant being who could perform miracles. All Deists were Unitarians in their understanding of God, but Unitarians rejected the notion that the single being of God was necessarily a distant being.

Chart 88

Christianity and the American Revolution

Christianity and the American Revolution

"The Revolutionary could no more admit a sovereign God than he could a sovereign king … Rulers henceforth rule only by the consent of the governed. The God of Puritanism, stripped of His antique power, had no recourse but to enter as a weakened prince into the temple of individualism and there to seek refuge."

Richard Mosier
The American Temper

Christianity and the American Revolution

"The biblical God celebrated by the Reformation was a monarch who elected his citizens and ruled his kingdom. The democratic god celebrated by the American people was a civil servant who was elected by the people to serve their interests. The biblical God was told he could remain in our company only so long as he stayed on the sidelines and served as a public mascot—not as an umpire, nor even as a player, but as a mascot."

Michael Horton
Made in America

At the level of national government, though it was never envisioned to be so at the state level, the unique truth claims of Christianity were never accepted and rarely tolerated. God was taken out of the public realm and reduced to the private realm of individual faith preferences. Christianity was the religion of the people because it garnered the most votes, not because it was true.

Chart 89

Christianity, the Federal Government, and State Government

Federal Government:

"Congress shall make no law respecting an establishment of religion, or prohibiting the free exercise thereof."
(Article I, Amendments to the Constitution)

State Government:

"Every person who shall be chosen a member of either house to any office or place of trust ... [shall] also make and subscribe the following declaration, to wit: "I do profess faith in God the Father, and in Jesus Christ His only Son, and in the Holy Ghost, one God, blessed for evermore; and I do acknowledge the holy scriptures of the Old and New Testament to be given by divine inspiration."
(Article 22, Constitution of Delaware [Sept 21, 1776])

It is most important to understand that the role of religion at the federal level was markedly different than that at the state level. The federal expression of religion was a least-common-denominator consensus— generalized beliefs that were held in common by the majority of people. This was not the case at the individual state levels where belief in Christian faith was often the standard for holding office. It seems that the states were often willing to embrace a weak view of religion at the highest level because they never envisioned a federal establishment that would overshadow and dictate to the states.

Chart 90

Charts of Ancient and Medieval Church History

The first of three books that survey the entire history of the church to the present day. Composed of maps, charts, and diagrams covering the initial fourteen centuries of the church, as well as theological ideas, trends, and outlines that can easily be used in the classroom.

ISBN 0-310-23316-X

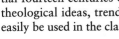

Charts of Bible Prophecy

This new addition to the ZondervanCharts series helps the student and specialist alike navigate through the many issues, themes, and different viewpoints of Bible prophecy. It does this in an even-handed way for side-by-side comparison.

ISBN 0-310-21896-9

Taxonomic Charts of Theology and Biblical Studies

Students as well as laypeople can see how the vast array of interrelated topics in theology and biblical studies fit together with this comprehensive collection of charts. A visual tracing of all major areas clarifies the connections and relationships between them.

ISBN 0-310-21993-0

Charts of Christian Theology and Biblical Studies

These precise summaries of concepts and arguments from the fields of historical and systematic theology introduce readers to important terms and positions. This handy reference allows students to organize and integrate material learned from a variety of textbooks and in the classroom.

ISBN 0-310-41661-2

Charts of the Gospels and the Life of Christ

Both students and Bible teachers will find this to be a vital reference tool, study source, and visual aid for New Testament study. It includes extensive charts on the life, ministry, setting, and teachings of Jesus Christ in three main categories: General Background, Chronological Charts, and Thematic Charts.

ISBN 0-310-22620-1

Chronological and Background Charts of the Old Testament

This revised edition of *Chronological and Background Charts of the Old Testament* includes forty-two new charts and eight revised charts. The charts cover historical, literary, archeological, and theological aspects of the Old Testament.

ISBN 0-310-48161-9

Chronological and Thematic Charts of Philosophies and Philosophers

This new edition of the popular *Philosophies and Philosophers* presents brief summaries of important philosophers and major ideas. Twenty-four two-color charts show how the various philosophies and philosophers are interrelated.

ISBN 0-310-46281-9

Charts of Cults, Sects, and Religious Movements

This resource presents well-organized, essential information on some of the most significant cults, sects, and religious movements that dot today's religious landscape. It gives both overview and detailed information on each group, including membership, worship practices, leaders, and publications.

ISBN 0-310-38551-2

Timeline Charts of the Western Church

The only comprehensive visual presentation of the history of the Western church in standard timetable format covering 4 B.C. to the present. In three sections, it supplies both summarized and detailed information, all in a time-tested, highly accessible column format.

ISBN 0-310-22353-9

Chronological and Background Charts of Church History

These eighty-one charts summarize the key people, events, dates, and ideas of church history. The index makes the book handy as a reference tool.

ISBN 0-310-36281-4

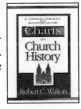

Chronological and Background Charts of the New Testament

Illustrates all aspects of chronology, historical background, and criticism of the New Testament. Topics include weights and measures, social structures, theories of the history of the text, history of Rome and Palestine, and more.

ISBN 0-310-41641-8

We want to hear from you. Please send your comments about this
book to us in care of zreview@zondervan.com. Thank you.

ZONDERVAN™

GRAND RAPIDS, MICHIGAN 49530 USA

W W W . Z O N D E R V A N . C O M

Installation Instructions

The Charts of Reformation and Enlightenment Church History *CD-ROM consists of PowerPoint presentations. If you do not have Microsoft PowerPoint® installed on your computer, the PowerPoint Viewer is included for your use.*

Windows®:

1. Insert the CD-ROM into your CD-ROM drive.
2. **If Microsoft PowerPoint is already installed on your computer:**
   a. Launch PowerPoint from your Start menu.
   b. You may be asked if you want to create a new presentation. If so, click Cancel.
   c. From the File menu, select Open and click on the "Look in" field at the top of the dialog box and select your CD-ROM drive. Select the appropriate charts and click "Open."
3. **If you do not have PowerPoint installed:**
   a. Click on the Start menu and select Run.
   b. Type "D:\ppview97.exe" (omit quotes and replace D with the letter of your CD-ROM drive if necessary) and press OK.
      (Note: If you do not know what the letter of your CD-ROM drive is, please double-click on My Computer. This gives you a list of all the drives on your computer. Your CD-ROM drive will have a little picture of a CD-ROM. Its letter is in parentheses.)
   c. This will start the installer for PowerPoint Viewer. Simply follow the onscreen instructions.
   d. Once installed, open the Microsoft PowerPoint Viewer 97 program from your Start menu.
   e. To open a file, click on the "Look in" field at the top of the dialog box and select your CD-ROM drive. Select the appropriate charts and click the "Show" button to begin the presentation.
4. To copy the files to your hard drive so that you can view the charts without the CD-ROM in the drive:
   a. Double-click on My Computer
   b. Right-click on your CD-ROM drive and choose Explore.
   c. Select all the files and select Copy from the Edit menu.
   d. Navigate to your hard drive and open the folder where you would like to place the files and select Paste from the Edit menu.

Macintosh®:

1. Insert the CD-ROM into your CD-ROM drive. If you have PowerPoint installed, skip to step 3. If you do not have PowerPoint installed, open the Microsoft PowerPoint 98 Viewer folder on the CD-ROM, then the Supporting Files folder. Double-click on the PowerPoint Viewer First Run icon to begin installation and follow the instructions on the screen.
2. Open the PowerPoint Viewer from your hard drive. Navigate to the CD-ROM from your desktop and select the appropriate chart file and click Open.
3. To open a file from PowerPoint, open the program (choose blank presentation and cancel for layout) and select Open from the File menu. Navigate to the CD-ROM from your desktop and select the appropriate charts and click Open.
4. To copy the files to your hard drive so you do not have to use the CD, simply select all the PowerPoint files, click-down, and drag them over to the folder on your hard drive where you would like to place them. Release the mouse button and they will begin to copy.